The Agile Enterprise

The Agile Enterprise

Applying Agile Principles to Drive Organizational Success

David Asch

BUSINESS EXPERT PRESS

Leader in applied, concise business books

The Agile Enterprise: Applying Agile Principles to Drive Organizational Success

First published in 2023 by
Business Expert Press, LLC
222 East 46th Street, New York, NY 10017
www.businessexpertpress.com

ISBN-13: 978-1-63742-547-3 (paperback)
ISBN-13: 978-1-63742-548-0 (e-book)

Business Expert Press Portfolio and Project Management Collection

First edition: 2023

10 9 8 7 6 5 4 3 2 1

For Laurie

Description

A group of eminent software developers gathered at a Colorado ski lodge in 2001, codifying *The Agile Manifesto*, a philosophy for efficiently accomplishing technical work. In this accessible, real-world-example-laden, and unexpectedly entertaining book, *The Agile Enterprise* explains how to apply The Agile Manifesto's ideas companywide.

The wisdom imparted in *The Agile Enterprise* teaches students to decompose large problems into manageable chunks, helps managers find their value among self-managing teams, and enables executives to measure and recognize success in their own Agile enterprises.

Keywords

applying the agile manifesto; agile development philosophy; how to build metrics in an agile environment; best practices for OKRs; managing agile projects; agile discovery

Contents

Testimonials

"Over the years, I have read multiple books on Agile methodologies. Some were quite good, but none was particularly entertaining. David possesses a unique gift. Not only does he make a compelling case for the use of Agile methodologies across departments in an organization, he does it through relatable examples and with immense humour. I continually found myself excited to move on to the next chapter, both for the educational value and for the raw entertainment. This is far and away the best book on Agile I have ever read."
—Pete Devenyi, (Retired) Senior Vice President, Global Products and Solutions, Dematic/Author, *Decoding Your Stem Career* (BEP 2022)

"For some recent time, many of the professionals involved in innovation projects, me included, have claimed to follow the guidelines of the Agile methodology. However, at the same time, they have often been aware that such claims were partially true. In his excellent book, David Asch provides an enlightening description of how the Agile Manifesto, originally founded on a theoretical basis, apparently tricky to apply, can be put into practice in simple and effective ways. Asch shows how Agile can really become a tool to improve the efficiency of a working group, be it the Engineering core team of a new startup looking for its place in the business or the HR department of a large company struggling to keep up with an increasingly competitive market.

Through simple and clear language, made up of examples, checklists, quizzes, and tutorials, the author intrigues you as a reader, and stimulates to review your way of dealing with daily work challenges, starting from the awareness of your own room for improvement. By overcoming the Waterfall model, instinctively and widely adopted, especially when under pressure, he shows how the more meticulous Agile approach based on broad overview, organization in micro tasks, strong synergy between teams and real-time evaluation of results through objectively measurable parameters, can effectively take your performance to a next level.

You will discover the importance of deeply comprehending one question and accurately estimating the effort for its possible resolutions. And you will appreciate the value of analyzing failures and raising red flags to prevent problems in the future. The Agile managerial mentality that Asch proposes is illuminating, not aimed at purely providing directions, instead more focused on understanding problems and paving the ways to teams' operations, according to a deep knowledge of collaborators and work context."—**Alessandro Ossoli, Chief Operating Officer, KoolSpan, Inc.**

"If you're a CEO, executive, or employee at a firm that wants to be more agile or that is already in the process, but things are not quite working out, this book is for you. Also, if you're interested in Agile, but think it's only something for tech companies or for people in IT, this book is also for you. David Asch explains that much of what Agile is about, has nothing to do specifically with software, but rather an approach and philosophy of how to tackle work.

One of the most notable aspects of this book is its accessibility. Even if you have no prior knowledge of Agile methodologies, the book does an exceptional job of explaining the basics in a way that is easy to understand. The case studies and real-world examples included in the book are also incredibly helpful. They provide a clear understanding of how Agile methodologies can be applied to a range of business functions, from marketing to HR to sales. I had honestly never thought about Agile for other business functions the way Asch does and he manages to do so with a great sense of humor.

I wish David Asch had written this book seven years ago and handed it to me. It would have saved me many headaches."—**Javier Ferraez, Product Management, Amazon.com**

Acknowledgments

Like many first-time authors, I didn't realize I had a book in me until others provided encouragement. The writing was an arduous process that I wouldn't have completed without the support of colleagues, friends, and family.

Interestingly, my most formative Agile experiences occurred long before Agile became a thing. The late Jim Carbonara, whom I cite in the book's introduction, provided a seminal Agile working environment early in my career. A few years later at a startup called Roadshow International, I worked for a superb Vice President of Engineering, Annie Bernstein, who instinctively broke big problems into small ones and had us work iteratively. The President and CEO of Roadshow, the late Don Soults, provided my first glimpse into executive-think when we'd hang out together working and kibitzing in the office on Saturdays. These early mentors and friends provided the base upon which I built my subsequent thinking and Agile practices.

The Business Expert Press team has been amazing. When Ed Stone reached out to ask if I was interested in writing an Agile book, I didn't take him seriously. However, Ed persisted and worked brilliantly to help me to create a viable outline and proposal. Ed introduced me to Managing Executive Editor, Scott Isenberg, who provided intelligent advice and immediate responses to my questions. Kam Jugdev and Tim Kloppenborg reviewed my proposal and delivered constructive, thoughtful feedback with a velvet hammer. Charlene Kronstedt provided expertise, helping me package the book, including her front cover design. The Exeter Premedia Services Private Ltd. team lent their eagle eyes, taking my manuscript and producing a cohesive book adhering to BEP standards.

When I finished writing a solid draft, I had two concerns. First, I didn't want to impose my tome on my friends/colleagues with busy jobs and full lives. Second, would I expose myself as a fraud by putting my work in front of people who know and live Agile? I needn't have worried.

My friends and colleagues were uniformly supportive. I am deeply grateful to Pete Devenyi, Alessandro Ossoli, and Javier Ferraez, who generously took the time to read the manuscript and write thoughtful testimonials.

Many people have wonderful spouses. Many writers have superb editors. Few are as fortunate as I am to have a wonderful spouse and superb editor rolled into one smart, beautiful package. My wife and best friend, Laurie Adler, has provided unequivocal spousal support and thoughtful, critical editing in equal measure. Not only does Laurie address my grammatical deficiencies, but she also challenges my ideas. All the mistakes in this book are mine, but Laurie's contributions immeasurably elevate the book's content and readability.

Introduction

Agility is the Holy Grail for today's corporations. Sleek, speedy, nimble, and athletic—who doesn't want that? That's why most CEOs boast about leading agile companies. Sadly, even though a CEO sees her business as an agile panther in the jungle, in most cases, it's more likely a clumsy, lumbering elephant, crashing into obstacles instead of adroitly avoiding them.

The term *Agile* comes from software development, where teams achieve success by undertaking small batches of work and fully completing them rather than engaging in months-long entire systems design sessions.

I came of professional age before anyone boasted about corporate agility and before Agile became formalized as a software development philosophy. During these ancient times, I experienced my first brush with Agile when I was a few years out of college in 1988.

I was a contractor working at the Office of Naval Research (ONR) in Ballston, Virginia. This was before the Metro was constructed when Ballston was a sleepy suburb. Mom & Pops dotted the streets, and it was easy to get terrific and inexpensive Mexican or Asian food for lunch.

I was assigned to the University Business Affairs division of the ONR, which administered research grants awarded to university professors. My sponsor was an affable 40-something guy named Jim, the Director of University Business Affairs. He explained that he wanted to build a software product for ONR personnel who manage and administer many grants at university field office sites.

Jim had a spacious office with a large desk, a credenza behind the desk with a desktop computer, and a small conference table. Jim's managerial job didn't require him to use the computer. This was in the days before most office workers were tethered to their computers. For the next year, I sat behind Jim's desk and worked at his computer while he selflessly sat at his conference table.

I came to the job with some mad dBase III Plus skills and used them to build the software. For those not of the 20th century, dBase III Plus was a pre-Windows, MS-DOS-based database management system that allowed a programmer to design data entry screens and navigation.

Nothing was magical about our routine, but we developed a steady cadence. Jim and I would chat about a piece of the product. Maybe he'd sketch out a couple of his ideas. I'd go code it up. dBase III Plus made it remarkably quick to translate an idea to the screen. When I had something demonstrable, Jim would take a look at the monitor, over my shoulder. Sometimes it was hours, sometimes a day or two. We iterated in this manner until he was satisfied with my work.

When we had a shippable (literally—this was pre-Internet days, and we used the post office) version, I'd write some documentation and installation instructions, Then I'd prepare floppy disks (I cannot recall if they were 5 1/4 or 3.5 inches) for each of the university sites. Jim and I would take trips to university field offices every few months to train users and listen to their suggestions.

Our road trips were especially memorable. Although Jim was in a managerial position and it behooved the workers at these sites to treat him nicely, it was obvious to me that everyone genuinely loved him. Since I had Jim's full support, even though my work was replacing their home-grown systems, I was treated mostly with kindness and acceptance—and occasional pushback. With Jim's encouragement, the government employees at these university sites worked with me to build features and workflow that enabled them to perform their jobs more efficiently.

This was Agile development on a small scale a decade before the *Agile Manifesto* was written. Jim created an environment where we worked shoulder-to-shoulder in an iterative process. We talked instead of writing complicated specifications for the work. We shipped working software at regular intervals and sought immediate feedback from end-users. Although Jim had probably never heard of the title, *Product Manager*, this was his role as well as *Subject Matter Expert*.

Under the eminently sensible guidance of my beloved mentor, Jim, we *did* Agile development before there *was* Agile development.

The subsequent popularization of Agile and Agile methodologies provided me the vocabulary, like *sprints* and *iterations*, to describe my early work at the ONR. The most interesting aspect of the experience was its naturalness. Jim and I fell into an efficient work partnership, with no special tools or methodologies to guide us.

I imagine the software luminaries who produced the *Agile Manifesto* a decade later were guided by the same principles Jim and I practiced. They merely formalized a set of ideas they were already following that seemed like old-fashioned common sense.

One of the key ideas in the *Agile Manifesto* is the suggestion to tackle large problems by breaking them into small, more easily accomplishable pieces. Finding large problems needing decomposition requires no imagination when real-life problems are ubiquitous.

Take, for example, the Internal Revenue Service (IRS), the government agency tasked with funding approximately everything the government does. The IRS operates a monolithic mainframe system running COBOL, a programming language that was already long-in-the-tooth in the 1980s.

Unsurprisingly, the IRS is having trouble finding COBOL programmers who are still alive. Equally unsurprisingly, the IRS has a long and unfruitful history of IT projects without end dates.

So, the IRS has a monumental challenge. With the weight of funding the entire U.S. government on its shoulders, there are probably many areas of the software that are so brittle, the IRS programmers are afraid to touch them when problems occur.

If anything screams for an Agile approach, it's the IRS's antiquated systems. By chipping away at pieces of the system, and replacing obsolete chunks with modern, well-built software, the IRS could slowly but predictably replace old with new. Instead, the IRS appears to be planning a *big bang* approach where they take years to design and implement a new system that invariably falls flat because it's outdated before it's unveiled.

I'm picking on the IRS because its immense problem illustrates the need for this book. Computing was in its infancy when the IRS designed its software. The software development process was modeled after building construction projects at that time.

Given the immense costs of making mistakes, building construction requires a fully approved architectural design before pouring the first drop of concrete. Unlike construction mistakes, software errors are inexpensive to repair when they're caught early. Still, it wasn't until the 21st century that software development philosophy diverged sharply from the construction project mindset.

Many corporate and government enterprise software projects are still mired in old-school thinking. Consequently, many modern software projects involve lengthy upfront design and documentation, followed by lengthy development, followed by lengthy testing. When the user finally receives the finished product, they may no longer be interested in the problems the software solves.

Fortunately, most companies don't face crises as gargantuan as the IRS. Still, a problem's a problem, and even the most well-run companies have them in spades. Over the course of my long career in small- to mid-sized commercial software companies, I've witnessed the success of Agile thinking across the board, not just for technical teams. Nontechnical departments like HR, Customer Support, Marketing, and Sales all benefit by approaching their work from an Agile mindset.

I started a consulting practice in 2020, 10xPrinciples, based on the idea that the best engineers are 10 times (10x) more effective than most of their colleagues. 10x performance isn't unique to engineers. Any high-performing company has superstar marketers, salespeople, magical customer support agents, and über-emotionally intelligent recruiters.

In the nature versus nurture debate, 10x performance demands a level of innate talent, but it also relies upon learned behavior. Teaching people to think and work in small chunks is one especially effective way to nurture 10x talent. I've found that skills like problem-solving and open-mindedness are just as important to 10x performance as having a first-rate technical toolbelt to draw from.

The most important aspect of my work at 10xPrinciples is helping companies apply Agile philosophies to all their intractable problems, not just the technical ones. With a base of Agile philosophy, a dollop of creativity, and several tablespoons of trust and collaboration, I've seen companies solve even their most complex problems.

Like many first-time authors, I questioned my qualifications before I embarked on writing this book. I began my career teaching math and computers at a private New England high school for a couple of years.

Although I loved teaching and vowed to return to it somehow, computers were my passion. I subsequently became a programmer, seeking and securing my first job as a contractor at the Federal Aviation Administration in Washington, DC, by phoning tech companies I found in the Yellow Pages. After a few years of government contracting, I decided to work at software companies in the private sector. Midway through my career, I started managing mostly Engineering and Product teams.

I've influenced cross-company processes at the executive level and applied the Agile principles I espouse in this book. Much like the cyclical nature of Agile projects, my career trajectory is circular. I began as a teacher and have become a teacher again, albeit not in the classroom.

One of the marvelous aspects of consulting is living the experiences I write about. My work is my laboratory. My especially experimental customers have taught me about failing fast, tweaking the variables, and trying again.

Agile is a philosophy. Most philosophies don't come with instructions about applying them to real life. Although the Agile philosophy isn't particularly esoteric, it doesn't prescribe behavior for actual work scenarios. This book is packed with examples and case studies that help illustrate Agile concepts and how they can be applied to real business problems. Some of the examples and case studies I include are loosely adapted from my real-life consulting engagements. The names and situations are changed to protect privacy.

When critics complain, "Agile doesn't work," they're usually knocking Agile methodologies like Scrum and not the Agile philosophy. As this book discusses in detail, in addition to teams fully internalizing the Agile philosophy, it's also important to take the useful pieces of methodologies and adapt them. Many of the Agile problems and solutions outlined in this book result from incorrect interpretations of Agile itself, heavy-handed processes, corporate dysfunction, or the inability to recognize success or failure.

For completeness, I present several methodologies that help teams to operationalize Agile concepts. There's nothing wrong with a methodology if it increases a team's effectiveness. But caveat emptor—tools and processes are at best a secondary distraction and at worst an obstacle. Like the Agile aficionados say, "Individuals and interactions over processes and tools." This book focuses on using Agile ideas to become a lean, mean, problem-solving team.

How to Read the Agile Enterprise

I hope this text is such a page-turner that readers consume the entire book in one big gulp, forgoing all other responsibilities and biological needs. At the same time, I also recognize this book is for harried people trying to get a leg up. Therefore, I acknowledge that some may pick and choose to read the parts of the book with the highest correlation to their most pressing problems.

Piecemeal readers, rejoice. Each chapter in *The Agile Enterprise* stands alone. Except for some case studies introduced in one chapter and referenced elsewhere, understanding a chapter is not predicated on absorbing the previous ones.

If terminology in a chapter is unclear, it was likely defined in an earlier chapter. A handy Glossary at the end provides definitions for every piece of business/technology jargon in the text.

CHAPTER 1

The Agility Myth

Agility is a positive word connoting nimbleness, speediness, and adaptability. Every CEO wants their company to be agile, and no CEO wants their company to be the opposite—lumbering, slow, and rigid. Yet few companies are truly agile.

Most companies aren't agile because developing cohesion between the Sales, Marketing, Human Resources, Product, and Engineering teams is difficult. While the leaders of each team are technically aligned as corporate representatives, their goals and objectives may be incompatible with their peers' goals and objectives. Before bemoaning a company's inflexibility or celebrating its sprightliness, a good first step is to examine executives' differing objectives.

The Mistaken CEO

The CEO of a publicly traded company may view her purpose as maximizing shareholder value. The same company's Chief Technical Officer (CTO) may see his role as delivering a technically sound software architecture. The head of Customer Success may say her job is to ensure that every customer has a good experience with the product and remains a customer.

Two interesting takeaways from the previous paragraph:

1. Three different leaders in the same company state three different raison d'êtres. One's mission depends on where one sits. People on the financial side of a business tend to focus on money. People on technology teams care about the nerdy engineering stuff. Customer-facing employees view their roles as an extension of customer happiness.
2. A *company* does not have goals. Indeed, a company cannot be *agile*. Only the *people* within a company may be agile. Only actual living,

breathing people have a purpose. The company is merely a legal construct with a Tax ID number. Although this may seem like splitting hairs, it's important to remember that a company is nothing more than an aggregation of great people who contribute their ideas and energy.

To maximize shareholder value, the CEO must make the company as profitable as possible. Companies profit when their customers clamor to buy the company's products. A CTO wants to build a robust software architecture that supports the products customers clamor to buy. The Customer Success Officer undoubtedly recognizes that helping customers solve their problems with the company's products leads to customer satisfaction. One of the coolest things about well-run companies is how all roads lead back to the customer.

Agile companies are responsive to their customers' ever-changing problems. Lumbering companies are slow to understand or acknowledge their customers' problems and deliver inappropriate solutions. Again, "agile companies" is merely shorthand for companies that employ a nimble workforce with some special qualities. The qualities required for agility are in short supply and, as a rule, are difficult to harness.

Every Rule Has Exceptions

Some companies have the prescience to conjure needs and desires before customers articulate them. Take Apple's invention of the iPod. Apple didn't invent digital music, nor did they invent portable music players; that distinction goes to Sony with their 1979 Walkman. Apple did, however, build an irresistibly beautiful device to store and play music while also providing a mechanism for monetizing and streaming music.

Apple created a solution to a problem customers couldn't articulate because they didn't have the right vocabulary. The popularity of the Walkman demonstrated a market for portable music. Apple riffed on the concept for the digital age.

Steve Jobs was a singularly unique CEO whose direct involvement in product development and design led Apple to greatness. He also ushered in a generation of Steve Jobs wannabe CEOs whose tone-deaf micromanagement hindered their companies' forward progress. Jobs was an outlier whose uniqueness has already been examined by terrific writers in thick biographies.

Rather than rehash Steve Jobs' genius, his approach to decision-making is germane to this agile discourse. A well-known example: Steve Jobs famously maintained a wardrobe of identical black turtlenecks and black jeans to avoid the cognitive overhead of deciding what to wear every morning. Did this make Jobs sartorially agile? Not really. The Jobs uniform was merely a way for him to avoid decision-making.

However, the point of this much-imitated Jobsian approach to small, personal decisions is that it freed him to focus on the important ones. The first principle of agility is classifying decisions by importance. Jobs classified his wardrobe as inconsequential, and he put it on autopilot. He regarded the user experience of the iPhone as super-important, demanding intense focus.

As the CEO of not just Apple, but Pixar as well, Jobs spread himself very thin. Add to this his insistence on controlling every aspect of the Apple product design and development, it's no wonder he wouldn't spare five seconds to consider his clothing. People like Jobs tend to understand all the decisions awaiting them, determine the ones they must solve themselves, and farm out the rest to others. It may seem like Apple was a one-man band, but Jobs was aided by a strong management team, each an expert in their area.

Apple is an exception to the agility myth. Even in the absence of Steve Jobs, the company continues to innovate. With a market cap of U.S.$2.8 trillion, Apple is unimaginably large and different from most of the rest.

Large Companies Are Vulnerable to Competition

Large companies that lack an enigmatic CEO have an understandably difficult time focusing on the most important decisions and changing course when necessary. It's hard enough for a romantic couple to stay in sync, much less expect everyone in an immense or even mid-sized company to march to the same beat.

The big players have the benefit of ample money, personnel, and other resources to overpower competitors even if they cannot outmaneuver them. However, even the mighty may fall when a large, unavoidable obstacle presents itself.

Two well-known examples:

1. *The Titanic* was a whiz-bang state-of-the-art ocean liner that sank on April 15, 1912, four days into her maiden voyage. The obstacle was an iceberg. The mighty Titanic could not avoid the obstacle and suffered unrecoverable damage to its hull. Students of history or those who watched James Cameron's eponymous Jack and Rose epic movie know the sad outcome.

2. *Kodak* was sitting pretty in the late 1970s, dominating the market in camera and film with sales nearing U.S.$10 billion. While Kodak wasn't blindsided by digital photography, its razors/razor blades business model is what doomed them. Kodak treated its cameras as a loss leader, using them to sell zillions of rolls of film later processed and printed on Kodak paper. Although they were marginally prepared for digital photography, Kodak filed for bankruptcy in 2012, without ever wrapping its head around the idea that people would digitally share photos instead of printing them (Brand Minds 2018).

The Titanic and Kodak faced vastly different situations, but both fell victim to immovable large objects. While the Titanic wasn't physically nimble enough to avoid its obstacle, Kodak lacked intellectual nimbleness. The common denominator of both is shared hubris and the belief they were too big to fail. The Titanic may have been lax about iceberg lookout, believing they could plow through anything. Ditto, Kodak with the digital photography onslaught.

The Darwinian business landscape is littered with once-great companies that couldn't adapt and became extinct. Business evolution is natural and expected. Nothing lasts forever.

More surprising is the graveyard of failed businesses with outstanding business models cut down in their youths before realizing their potential to become household names. Smaller companies may lack the size advantages of the Goliaths, but smallness promotes easier communication, faster decision-making, and easier pivoting.

Armchair quarterbacking the failures of smaller companies with stellar business plans is easy because ivory tower punditry is a bloodless sport. The real, bloody challenge is fighting in the trenches for a company's survival. That is, nothing is easy about succeeding in business even with the best ideas and the best teams.

Startups are typically staffed by young idealistic people willing to work punishing hours for an uncertain future. Older employees may buy into the company's vision but have family responsibilities requiring a steady paycheck and preventing them from making the same time commitment. The danger of attracting solely young employees, or hiring a homogenous workforce, is the absence of diversity. Diversity in business isn't a Woke concept—it's necessary to have employees of all shapes, sizes, ages, ethnicities, races, and genders to ensure broadly reasoned, well-considered decisions.

Potential employees understandably prefer to join rocket ships, not Titanics. Identifying a business with the best chance for success is too important for a potential employee to flip a coin. How should outsiders discern the winners from the losers? For that matter, how should company leaders determine if they are assiduously addressing their challenges?

Agility Checklist

An Agility Checklist provides a *deceptively* simple way to determine if a company can roll with the punches—absorb glancing blows, duck knockout punches, learn from mistakes, and have fun along the way.

Table 1.1 Agility Checklist

	Capability	Description	Yes/No?
1	Vision	Are leaders in place who articulate the raison d'être of the company—why its idea is the best, why the best people are in place, and how to best execute the business plan?	
2	Communication	Are executives effectively communicating the company vision and also explaining how individual teams will contribute to the endeavor?	

(Continues)

(*Continued*)

	Capability	Description	Yes/No?
3	Cohesion	Is there employee buy-in and understanding of the vision? The best way to determine this is to ask employees about the company's purpose.	
4	Measurement	Does the company know how to differentiate success from failure? Ideally, no work is ever undertaken without also establishing a way to measure success.	
5	Experimentation	Is there a culture of experimentation? Since no team has all the answers, the employees need the capability to run short, controlled experiments.	
6	Risk-taking	Is failure accepted? There's plenty written about failing fast and learning from mistakes. Failure is often slow and agonizing. An appetite for healthy risk-taking without recrimination for failure often results in breakthroughs.	
7	Diversity	Is the company diverse? Every aspect of diversity—ethnicity, gender, race, religion, sexuality, age, economic—leads to better-considered decision-making.	
8	Judiciousness	Do the decision-makers in the company have wisdom? A challenge for youthful startups is youthful decision-making without the benefit of experience. This isn't suggesting that old fogeys occupy the executive suite, but some "old souls" are essential regardless of age.	

How Did Your Company Fare?

0–2 Yeses—Not gonna lie, your company may suffer from unenlightened management. However, the first step in fixing a problem is acknowledging it. If you can effect change in your company, it's time to marshal the troops and chip away at the problems.

3–6 Yeses—Most of the respondents who candidly answer probably fall into this happy middle. Things aren't terrible, but there's room for improvement.

7–8 Yeses—Congratulations! Your company is perfect. Maybe you shouldn't have paid for this book because you don't need it. Joking, of course. Even the finest organizations have dysfunction if one examines their nooks and crannies. Look more closely, amigo!

Fixing the Problems

The problem with a checklist like this one is it raises deep, complicated issues and requests glib Yes/No answers. The answers to just about all these questions are nuanced and often subjective.

The questions in this Agility Readiness checklist contain enough ambiguity that many of the answers are probably like, "I'm not really sure—kinda, sorta, I guess." If so, not to worry. Many of these items are aspirational for most companies. Being aware of the capabilities is the first step in developing the necessary agility muscles.

Still, the Agility Checklist should provide a general feeling of whether your company is in the agility-ready ballpark. Most of the items cannot be fixed by snapping one's fingers or issuing an edict from on high. However, with some effort, thoughtful, hard-working managers can articulate a vision, communicate it to employees, and ensure that everyone is rowing the boat in the same direction. Some of the other items are cultural and must be understood and demonstrated by the management team.

If colleagues compare their agility assessments, answers will probably vary wildly. Differing assessments of agility reflect an important point. Wouldn't it be terrific if the different departments in a company behaved like independent human organs working cooperatively to keep their human host alive? But get real. Yes, everyone in the company is motivated to seek success for the company. But the cooperative organs within the human body aren't subject to office politics, kingdom building, information hoarding, and self-defeating behavior. The human organs operate independently from the human brain with emotions, jealousy, and squirrely pettiness.

Piecemeal Agile

Now is the time to differentiate Agile from agile. The adjective *agile* is merely an appealing word to which virtually every company aspires. Agile with a capital *A* is a different animal referencing an entire software development philosophy.

Leave it to the software developers. For all their professed iconoclasm, software folks know a savvy marketing hook when they see one. Taking a philosophy and labeling it *Agile* brilliantly frames a concept that holds universal appeal.

From this point on, the software philosophy is called capital-A, *Agile* and the adjective meaning speedy and nimble is lowercase *agile*.

Software teams in many companies practice some form of Agile. However, the practice of a software philosophy doesn't mean this team has any special enlightenment that's lacking in the rest of the company. A software team utilizing Agile software methods isn't necessarily more agile than any other team in the company.

Meeting the Implications of Agility

The capabilities in the Agility Checklist (FYI: Agility is capitalized here because it's a formal name, not a software philosophy) are easy to understand and devilishly difficult to implement. Companies tend to succeed when they serve a preexisting need or create a new desire and execute better than anyone else. Winning seems so simple, but it requires all the factors in the Agility Checklist. Shortcomings in these capabilities tend to get in the way of success.

Virtually all the capabilities in the Agility Checklist require cooperation among humans. The idea of people working well together may feel like a quaint concept in this age of artificial intelligence (AI) and machine learning (ML). Rest assured, although AI/ML will impact jobs and careers, building a successful company cannot be left to machines alone. Humans working alongside machines must tackle the communication, risk-taking, and challenges of judiciousness that make or break companies.

People can talk a blue streak, process complicated ideas, and evaluate different opinions. Yet, effective communication is perhaps the biggest barrier to success. Why is communication so difficult? When companies begin, communication is easy. A startup company may fit into a garage with so few people sitting close together it is almost impossible *not* to communicate.

Case Study: The Burger Shack

Suppose two beach-bum friends start up a burger stand at the beach. They share a vision of high-quality burgers at a fair price. They also want a lifestyle enabling them to surf every morning and make enough money to afford their rent. They set up a grill in a little hut with a window where they serve lunch to customers. When the friends begin, they offer hamburgers, cheeseburgers, lettuce, tomato, onion, pickles, ketchup, and mustard. That's it. The two friends have plenty to juggle between managing their vendors, deliveries, food preparation, cooking, and finances.

Demand grows as their reputation builds for quality and price. Lines go around the corner, and it's hard for the two friends to keep up. They decide to take some of their profits and hire two additional staff to help prepare, cook, and serve food. The company has just doubled in size. What began as shorthand between the like-minded friends now must be explicitly communicated to the two workers. It's still manageable.

The business continues to thrive. Word of mouth and some excellent restaurant reviews bring in people from far-flung locations. Customers want more. They request french fries, milkshakes, and hot dogs. The crowds are great for business but annoying for customers waiting outside in line for upward of an hour. When they finally get their food, customers complain the limited outdoor seating is already taken. Customers request indoor seating to eat their food instead of just a carry-out window with weather-dependent seating. They want the restaurant to open for longer hours so they can come for either lunch or dinner.

The two friends are at a crossroads. Although they're happy with their business as-is, they see sales plummet on rainy or cold days when customers are unwilling to wait outside in discomfort. To satisfy customer demands, they must enlarge their menu, increase business hours, and find a location that accommodates sit-down dining. Any one of these changes complicates their original idea. The would-be burger kings decide to go for broke, quadrupling their staff and securing loans to cover their up-front expenses.

In the process of becoming business moguls, the two beach bums have too much going on to manage every aspect of the restaurant. Still, they want to retain their original ideas of quality and value. However, instead of having an implicit understanding, the founders must communicate their vision through a new management layer.

Without belaboring the Burger Shack example, it's easy to imagine how everything becomes more complicated as businesses achieve levels of success and grow larger. For restaurants, growth often means opening additional locations and possibly franchising. New teams form to address the different restaurant functions like waitstaff, procurement, cuisine, and finance. Each team may have different objectives and different locations. What used to be an implicit understanding because everyone was in the same room now must be communicated over Zoom in a company all-hands meeting from all the various locations. As companies grow and expand on the original simple idea, the message and vision become diffuse, sometimes to the point that employees no longer share a common understanding of the purpose of the business.

The burger example is at once familiar, but it also raises plenty of questions. The familiar part is the tale of two beach bums who never aspire to greatness but somehow fall into it. The unlikely success of the founders changes the nature of their problems. Cracks in agility are most evident when organizations experience growth.

Burger Shack Agility Checklist

The fast-growing Burger Shack may be a success on paper. However, the business is undergoing many predictable stresses. A second viewing of the Agility Checklist from earlier with Burger Shack-specific issues and mitigations illustrates how a fledgling business positions itself for positive growth.

Table 1.2 Burger Shack Agility Checklist

	Capability	Burger Shack Problem	Mitigation
1	Vision	The founders had the original vision of quality and value. Now that the business has expanded, the original vision doesn't really apply to some aspects of the business, like the waitstaff or managing the complicated maze of suppliers and fulfillment. There is no longer a vision that unifies the entire enterprise.	This is one of those Kumbaya times when management needs to come together to consider the business in its entirety. If the founders are lacking in this vision, it's possible they're not up to the task of running this new company.
2	Communication	Managers are now in charge of different parts of the business—kitchen, serving, menu, finance, ordering, and expansion. Although each manager is part of the Burger Shack team, they have different criteria for success and different incentives. For example, the waiters may be incentivized to increase the total ticket by upselling fries and other non burger options, drinks, and desserts; this has nothing to do with quality or value.	Setting objectives specific to each manager's area of business is fine. However, these objectives must be unified and complementary.
3	Cohesion	Employees are unable to articulate why their jobs at Burger Shack are special. Many, when answering anonymously, state, "It's a job with a paycheck, no more no less." The food buyers may still be committed to sourcing the finest foods from local farmers, but this isn't something the front-line workers even know about.	Management's most important mission is to communicate the same message to employees regardless of their jobs or stations. Leadership should inspire pride in the company and the importance of each person to the mission. In this case, educating front-line workers about the farm-to-table aspects of the business illustrates the uniqueness of Burger Shack and may become a source of pride in the mission.

(Continues)

(*Continued*)

	Capability	Burger Shack Problem	Mitigation
4	Measurement	The founders never built tools to measure the effectiveness of their decisions. Instead, they made their decisions based purely on what they liked. They continue to view measurement as *too corporate* and still take a gut-level approach to decision-making. Rather than understanding their sales numbers at a detailed level, the founders just care about their net profit. Therefore, they have no idea how a big change like increasing their hours might affect the business because they have no concept of tracking sales totals by the hour, tracking the food items that are popular at different times, or myriad other measurements that help to understand the business at a microlevel.	The need to measure instead of going with gut-level decision-making is a cultural shift that needs to come from the top. If the leaders of the company insist on nonscientific thinking, it's likely they will make costly mistakes.
5	Experimentation	Burger Shack has lost a significant amount of money chasing customer suggestions that didn't pan out. For example, they increased their hours only to find that their dinner traffic was light without a license to serve alcohol. When the founders started serving french fries, they adhered to their values and tried to buy high-quality ingredients at a good price. However, they didn't spend time trying out different oils and experimenting with hand-cutting potatoes.	As the restaurant expands to multiple locations, experimentation is easy and important. Instead of committing, testing the waters with easily reversible experiments enables the teams to rapidly cycle through ideas and commit to the best ones.

	Capability	Burger Shack Problem	Mitigation
6	Risk-taking	Given that there's little culture of experimentation, there's also little appetite for trying and failing. The business impact of failures is considered too detrimental to take big risks. When the founders decided to sell french fries, they invested U.S.$10,000 in an industrial fryer. Although they were reasonably certain they'd make their money back, they figured they could withstand the loss if it didn't pan out. They didn't view the french fryer as a big risk. When a signage vendor visited the Burger Shack, she told them a large, neon sign affixed to the roof would pay for itself in two years with the increased foot traffic it would bring. The founders passed on this because they didn't want to spend the money on something they didn't view as a sure thing.	Much like measurement, risk-taking is a cultural value that must come from conscious management. That is, managers must decide that they welcome fast failure and will reward rather than penalize new ideas—even the ones that fail. For decisions like expensive signage, a risk-taking organization devotes research time to better understand how signage and advertising help to grow similar businesses. Smart companies take calculated risks where they believe the odds for success are in their favor based on the data they've evaluated.
7	Diversity	The company is still led by the two founders, both like-minded, young, White males. The management team consists mostly of their homogeneous friends.	Until the management team diversifies, they are subject to groupthink. The lack of diversity stymies progress, especially as the business considers expanding into neighborhoods or cuisines that the management team doesn't understand.
8	Judiciousness	There's little disagreement between the management team and the founders because they have similar outlooks. This makes a fun, harmonious environment for the management team.	Blanket agreement is problematic. No, management teams shouldn't fight to the death in a cage match, but the lack of dissension reflects a lack of judiciousness. This is where broader, less nepotistic hiring is important.

The Delicate Balance of Process

The Burger Shack example is typical of many businesses. The two founders had a good formula and great chemistry and successfully navigated through the initial startup phase. Growing the business requires a level of management agility the team does not currently possess. If the founders get a team on board with diverse viewpoints and experiences, Burger Shack stands a good chance of successful growth.

Starting and growing a business isn't for the faint of heart. Look at almost any successful business that began with two or more cofounders, and a few years out, at least one of them will invariably be acrimoniously out the door. The intense stress of running a business, from money problems to people problems, is enough to break up most partnerships. It doesn't help that many startups are begun by people barely beyond childhood who lack sufficient frontal lobe development to navigate both business decisions and interpersonal relationships.

For example, the two Steves, Jobs and Wozniak, parted ways early on due to philosophical differences. Bill Gates and Paul Allen also got a quickie divorce. Ben and Jerry, still friends after their exit to Unilever, are the exceptions to the rule of failed partnerships. Perhaps Ben and Jerry succeeded because they were older when they began their company and had a mature, lifelong friendship. Or maybe ice cream is less stressful than the computer biz.

When companies start going off the rails, investors frequently step in, demanding the youthful founders hire some seasoned veterans. The proverbial "adults in the room."

The challenges of hiring older managers:

1. Older managers bring preconceived ideas about how to tame unruly companies. The taming of unruly companies often ushers in new processes—formulas and dictates to put some structure around the work—this sure doesn't sound like much fun.
2. Older managers are often less fun and raucous than youngsters.

Process heaviness is a term that generally means: The hoops to jump through to meet the process are more onerous than the problem it's attempting to solve. Introducing new processes to a company is a delicate act of needle-threading. Although companies shouldn't be governed as dictatorships, neither should they be democracies where everyone gets an equal vote. Still, for new processes to be accepted, the affected employees must buy into them. Processes seldom succeed when they are inflicted upon employees by senior management without worker buy-in.

Companies achieve agility by introducing sensible processes that *fit the business*, not vice versa. It never works to take a boilerplate process from a business management guide and mold the company around the process. Seasoned managers who join a company first spend time getting the lay of the land before making any changes. These enlightened managers become acquainted with employees' skills and aspirations and solicit their opinions since many of the best ideas come from the bottom up.

Key Takeaways

1. Even though they're all on the same management team, leaders in any company have different goals and different measures for success.
2. Seeking customer satisfaction is the common denominator that coalesces leaders who have different objectives.
3. Agile companies are quick to recognize and pivot when their solutions do not adequately address their customers' problems.
4. Non-agile companies are slow, lumbering, and unable to recognize the need to change course.
5. Apple under Steve Jobs is an example of an agile company.
6. Most companies are nothing like Apple.
7. Companies that don't meet enough of the criteria for agility may successfully emerge from their startup phase but will face growth problems.
8. Increasing corporate agility requires some combination of process change, culture change, and possibly personnel change.
9. Every company is unique. A process that works for one company won't necessarily work for another company.
10. Smart managers understand the needs of their company and build processes to fit, not vice versa.

CHAPTER 2

Brief Tour of Agile Software Development

A February 2001 gathering of 17 legendary software developers at a Wasatch Mountain, Utah ski resort, resulted in a set of ideas so ground-breaking that they named it the *Agile Manifesto*. Since the ski resort attendees gathered to have some fun with their friends, they likely never imagined the global impact of their after-dinner bull session on the software development profession (Highsmith 2001).

When many of us hear the term *Manifesto*, we may think of Marx's and Engels's fiery rhetoric in *The Communist Manifesto*, which laid the ideological groundwork for socialism. Comparatively, *The Agile Manifesto* is surprisingly brief and gentle. Nowhere in the *Agile Manifesto* do its authors call for the "forcible overthrow of all existing social conditions" demanded by Marx and Engels (Marxist Internet Archive n.d.). Although the *Communist Manifesto* may be one of the world's most influential political documents, the *Agile Manifesto* is plenty important within the world of software development.

The Agile Manifesto

The *Agile Manifesto* is concise:

"We are uncovering better ways of developing software by doing it and helping others do it.
    Through this work we have come to value:
        1. Individuals and interactions over processes and tools
        2. Working software over comprehensive documentation
        3. Customer collaboration over contract negotiation
        4. Responding to change over following a plan

That is, while there is value in the items on the right, we value the items on the left more."

(Beck et al. 2001)

Principles of the Agile Manifesto

The *Agile Manifesto*'s authors also published a set of 12 underlying guiding principles (Beck et al. 2001). Instead of reprinting the principles, the following bullets capture the high points of the *Agile Manifesto*:

- **Deliver working software**—There's no better way to collaborate with customers and other stakeholders than to give them something to see and touch. Even if each release is small, establishing a regular cadence of software delivery opens the door to continuous feedback.
- **Expect change**—As a Programming team scurries around writing software, the world doesn't stop. Deals are won and lost. Senior management comes and goes. New opportunities arise. The needs of a robust business change much faster than the cycle of delivering a finished software product. Architecting a solution with the expectation it will change is eminently more sensible than hoping for an unchanging business landscape.
- **No handoffs**—The collaborative nature of Agile development is antithetical to the notion of Product Management handing Engineering a brain dump and leaving them to their own devices. Furthermore, Engineering doesn't toss a completed product over the fence for Quality Assurance's blessing. The Product, Engineering, and Quality Assurance teams work side-by-side from start to end, communicate constantly, and work iteratively.
- **Sustainability**—Nope, this isn't about saving electricity or shifting to nonfossil fuels. With Agile, teams must create schedules, enabling them to *sustainably* maintain a constant pace. A sustainable pace is achieved by building in periods of heads-down work, periods of information gathering, and

periods of reflection. Avoiding antipatterns like 80-hour weeks because they are *unsustainable* is a key to maintaining a steady pace.

- **Self-management**—The team takes responsibility for its working style, standards, and deliverables. Trusting Agile teams to take responsibility is the way to best ensure they invest themselves fully in the project.

Review of the Agile Manifesto

With an understanding of the *Manifesto's* underlying principles, it's time to dig into the meanings of its four simple rules. As its creators state, they place more value on the left-hand side of each statement but still heed the right-hand side.

1. **Individuals and interactions over processes and tools**—Remember, the authors of the *Agile Manifesto* are renowned software developers. They recognize that software development is equal parts art and science. Although processes and tools may provide an assist, the way to solve difficult problems and deliver elegant solutions requires the constant collaboration of teammates. It's fine if a tool or process helps to facilitate the project, but there's no substitute for whiteboarding and talking through complicated problems.

2. **Working software over comprehensive documentation**—The measure of a successful project is the software. If the software robustly solves its users' problems, everyone can go on vacation and celebrate a job well done. Internal documentation is especially important to capture an institutional memory of the software's inner workings, design considerations, and caveats. If the team successfully delivers an intuitive, simple product, user documentation can be lightweight, covering only the areas of potential confusion.

3. **Customer collaboration over contract negotiation**—A constant feedback loop results from delivering small-batch chunks of working software. Although there's probably a contract in place with a customer stating the parameters of the work, the final product is always

better if it accommodates steady feedback, which invariably differs from the letter of the contract.

4. **Responding to change over following a plan**—Flexibility is the key to virtually any business project. A plan is merely a set of forethoughts imagined by businesspeople before the project begins. When the circumstances of the business change or the iterative development gives customers new and better ideas, it's time to modify the plan. As Mike Tyson says, "Everyone has a plan until they get punched in the mouth." Tyson means having a game plan is fine, but be ready to change it when reality intercedes.

What's the Big Deal About Agile?

This Agile stuff seems perfectly sensible, right? To modern ears, Agile is common sense. Software engineering didn't start in earnest until the 1970s. Most colleges and universities didn't even have computer science majors until the mid to late 1980s. Therefore, the *Agile Manifesto* authors were the pioneers.

The Agile software movement replaced a software development approach called *Waterfall*. Based on building construction, the Waterfall method takes a radically different approach than Agile. Imagine pouring the concrete, laying a building's foundation, and building the walls, only to learn the building is pointed in the wrong direction.

There's no room for *winging it* in building construction. The architectural plan for the entire building must be created, scrutinized, modified, and approved before anyone even thinks about construction. The plan must be followed to a tee. Any deviations from the plan result in costly redoing of work.

Software is completely different from building construction. The cost of deviating from a building construction plan is potentially immense, even life-threatening. The stakes of deviating from a software plan are significantly lower. Yet, Waterfall was the accepted method for software development before Agile overtook Waterfall. The software highway is littered with failed Waterfall projects. Yet, Waterfall projects are still being initiated.

A Brief Tour of Waterfall Development

Understanding Waterfall is the only way to appreciate Agile's revolutionary nature. Like a real-life waterfall, there's only one way down and, hopefully, you don't crash into the rocks at the bottom. Waterfall is all about handoffs. A Planning team begins a Waterfall project by mapping out all the screens, all the interactions, all the system architecture, and everything else about the project. The upfront planning process is understandably long and arduous. The weight and thickness of the resulting documentation depend on the size of the project, but Waterfall project documentation is typically voluminous.

The Programming team gets to work after the Design team delivers a document. Since the document spells out everything in excruciating detail, there are few reasons for the document's authors to interact with the programmers. The programmers build against the specification they have received and work until completion. Then, the Testing team takes the finished release and scrutinizes it. The programmers fix any issues, and the software is released to customers.

What are the chances of success from the Waterfall method? It depends on how one defines success. Waterfall projects may succeed if success is measured by the delivery of a documentation tome and a product that slavishly follows the specification.

The Waterfall method tends to fall apart when success is measured by how well the software solves a customer's problems. The Waterfall process of handing off without circling back and iterating almost guarantees an ill-fitting solution to a problem that may no longer even exist.

Is There Anything Good About Waterfall?

Although Waterfall has been mostly debunked as an unacceptable software methodology, remember that nothing is ever 100 percent good or evil. The tortuous upfront Waterfall design process does provide a holistic understanding of the system. Sometimes the Agile approach of chipping away at a problem with iterative deliverables results in an incomplete understanding of the whole.

As an example of Waterfall versus Agile, imagine an autonomous ride-share startup, *JustTrustMe*, with a shoestring budget, trying to compete with Uber and Lyft. Since JustTrustMe can't yet afford developers, they outsource their Web app to a mobile development company. The budget-conscious JustTrustMe requests pricing and time estimates from their contractor.

The contractor may respond:

> We're unsure how long it will take because we don't yet understand what you need. Give us a month to work with your team so that we can sketch out a preliminary set of low-fidelity flow diagrams that reflect the entire website. After we complete this work and you review it, we'll be able to provide pricing and time estimates.

Isn't the contractor proposing a Waterfall project to holistically understand the landscape? Not exactly. The contractor needs to learn enough about the project to size and price it. The diagrams they produce reflect a general understanding of the entire application but lack a detailed understanding of any of it.

One of the misconceptions about Agile is that working iteratively on small chunks of functionality means it's unnecessary to possess a high-level understanding of the system as a whole and how the pieces will ultimately fit together. Gaining a high-level understanding should never require a multi-month or years-long design cycle, but it requires a rapid, up-front discovery period.

Weaknesses of Waterfall

Waterfall, oh Waterfall. How do I hate thee? Let me count the ways:

1. **Assumption of stasis:** An oft-used "time is passing us by" device in movies shows the main character walking along, while everyone else around them is frozen in time. A snap of the fingers starts everyone up again, unaware of the break in the time continuum. Waterfall assumes the business problems being addressed remain unchanged during a long design process. More realistically, the problems that

existed at the beginning of the design process will be entirely replaced by new and different problems by the end of the design process.

2. **No feedback loop:** The long handoff cycle of completed work from one team to another compounds the magnitude of mistakes. Imagine a finished product delivered to a customer after a multi-year Waterfall process that no longer serves their needs. The absence of an iterative, cyclical process means that customers couldn't opine about early-stage functionality to nip problems in the bud. Even if the Development team followed the design specification to a tee, if the spec is wrong, so is everything else.

3. **Quality control of large batch development:** Imagine a small craft brewery that produces award-winning India Pale Ales (IPAs) and stouts. The brewery is acquired by a national brand determined to make the beer available countrywide. Somehow, the beer doesn't taste as good as before, and whatever gave it its uniqueness in small batches cannot be replicated on a large scale. It may be a matter of micromanaging small-batch brewing along the way.

   For example, the brewmaster may taste an interim batch and decide to make slight changes to subtly improve quality. By improvising instead of adhering to a recipe, a small-batch brewer responds to minute differences in the hops, malt, and barley to create a unique and delicious batch each time.

   These extemporaneous beer brewing changes become more difficult in large-scale production because consumers expect consistency. With Agile, chipping away at a big feature set in short, iterative work cycles is akin to small-batch brewing. The brew master's quick modifications to improve quality are conceptually identical to a team changing direction after a sprint. Small batch software promotes easier quality control than large batch software because short delivery cycles enable developers to incorporate customer feedback and make small modifications.

   A multi-month Waterfall software development effort is like large batch brewing. Testing large batch software is more difficult than small batch testing because of the sheer size and greater number of features, and the lack of small batch checks and balances along the way. Small batch software is easier to test and fix than large batch software for a couple of reasons. For one, small batch testing goes faster because there are fewer conditions to explore. Additionally, when bugs are discovered in testing small batch work, the code is still at the forefront of developers' minds, making the fixes easier.

Throwing the Baby Out With the Bathwater

The idiomatic expression, "throwing out the baby with the bathwater," reflects the kneejerk attitude that if an idea is partially incorrect, it's best to eliminate the entire idea. When a shiny, new idea replaces an old, debunked idea, it takes time for the pendulum to return to the sensible middle ground. Such is the case with Agile and Waterfall.

Although the Agile approach of chipping away at a problem, doubling back, and regularly reevaluating is more sensible than the Waterfall approach, Agile zealotry is unwise.

Employing a Waterfall process, home builders closely scrutinize the architect's plans before moving on to construction. There's no room for an architect to half design a building, and *wing it* on the rest as the building takes shape.

Constructing software is different from constructing buildings. However, some aspects of software require an upfront complete understanding before moving forward. For example, suppose a Software team is building a new architectural framework for a company's suite of products. Even though it's unnecessary to exhaustively design each architectural component at the outset, it's vitally important to understand the full set of requirements. Although an upfront *big think* isn't precisely a Waterfall methodology, it is *Waterfall-ish*.

Misunderstanding the Agile Manifesto

One of the challenges with manifestos, including the *Agile Manifesto*, is that instruction manuals don't typically accompany them. Although the *Agile Manifesto's* authors included their set of guiding principles, these principles are open to interpretation. For example, one could interpret the *Working Software Over Comprehensive Documentation* tenet to mean it's far better to build something that works instead of writing about how it should work. While working software is better than great documentation, it doesn't mean the documentation is optional. That is, accomplishing the first tenet of a principle doesn't obviate the need for the second. A common-sense reading of the Agile Manifesto and its guiding principles isn't a heavy lift because its language is simple, and its concepts are clear. However, applying these principles to the rough and tumble of actual work is devilishly difficult.

The following scenario illustrates how a team might misinterpret the Agile Manifesto and fail to achieve its objectives: A grocery store technical team is tasked to build an e-commerce website for online shopping.

All the stakeholders may agree on a general understanding of the components required for an online shopping website. In the interest of delivering working software, the team wants to deliver software quickly with minimal interference. The technical team asks their customers to choose the most important piece of the application as a starting point. There's general agreement that selecting grocery items into a basket is most important. The developers confer with the product managers and start coding away. Lickety-split, the team produces the fundamentals of selecting items and creating shopping carts. In a demo, customers have a few suggestions but are enthusiastic about the speedy delivery of a work-ing piece of software.

The customers next request a product search capability. Once again, the developers discuss as a team and produce a search feature in record time. The presentation doesn't go so smoothly when customers review the search feature. For one, the search requires fuzzy matching instead of an exact match. For example, *fruit roll-ups* isn't recognized because it's *fruit rollups* in the database. The team also neglects to build any filtering capabilities. For example, typing *mango* brings up fresh mangos, mango juices, mango ice creams, and mango face creams, and the user is forced to wade through hundreds of products without a way to refine the search.

The point of this grocery example isn't to delve into the minutiae of an e-commerce website. It's to point out that Agile development requires plenty of planning, design, and forethought while also engag-ing with users. Agile is more a way to focus on small pieces than a shortcut. So, when the *Agile Manifesto* states, "Customer collaboration over contract negotiation," it's not a zero-sum sentence. Yes, customer collaboration is paramount, but there's also a set of behaviors to which both sides must agree.

The Agile Industry

The *Agile Manifesto* creators penned the behaviors they already followed. What seemed revolutionary to the larger software world was, to the creators, merely business as usual. Therefore, Kent Beck, Martin Fowler, and other software celebrities on the ski trip probably didn't imagine their ideas about Agile development would spawn the burgeoning industry.

The translation of philosophical ideas into concrete steps is called a *methodology*. The methodologies invented to make the *Agile Manifesto* approachable are each quite different, but they all have the same goals— to deliver all the goodies of the *Agile Manifesto*—working software built in a collaborative environment with enough wiggle room to turn on a dime and respond to changes.

Although there are plenty of comprehensive books about each Agile methodology, here's a quick and handy guide that hits some of the high points of each.

Scrum

Scrum is such a well-known methodology that many people incorrectly consider it synonymous with Agile. Scrum is built around *user stories*, which is a whimsical name for a feature that Engineering will build. User stories, however, have a specific format:

As a [WHO—user persona], I want to [WHAT—explain the action] so that [WHY—express the reason]

Using our grocery scenario from before, here are a few user story examples:

- As a grocery shopper with a broken leg, I want to order my groceries online so that I can maintain my independence without having to pester my daughter to shop for me.
- As a grocery shopper, I want to search for items I need to save time from having to page through every food item on the website.
- As a grocery shopper, I want to filter the results of my searches when too many items appear so that I can easily see the ones I care about.

There are a few important points to understand about these user stories:

1. These stories express a shopper's needs instead of a website administrator's. Often, there are several different types of users of the same system, and it's important to identify each feature's intended audience.

2. These stories are quite general and provide no details about implementing these features. By keeping stories vague, the stakeholders must discuss them to better understand users' motivations, acceptable outcomes, and myriad other details. User stories are merely a starting point.

3. These example stories are expressed simply but may be too large to implement. The person with the broken leg in the first story requests an entire website. The goal of each story is to explain a need that can be fulfilled within a reasonable amount of time. When user stories are too unwieldy, writing more focused stories is best.

4. The *Why* part of the story is key. If the story writer omits the reason for the request, the Development team should smell blood in the water and become piranhas. Sometimes the *why* is omitted because the story creator doesn't know the users' reason for the request. Before this story moves forward, the creator should return to the source and get more information. Implementing user stories without solid *whys* leads to unnecessary development or software that doesn't adequately address the users' needs.

There's an art and science to writing effective user stories, and these tips just touch the surface. Once the team has an acceptable set of stories and the engineers understand them, the engineers size the stories relative to one another based on their estimation of the implementation time for the story. One common approach to sizing stories is to assign a prime number between 1 and 11 (1, 3, 5, 7, 11) to each story where a *1* is trivial, and an *11* is exceedingly time-consuming. If the engineers attempt to assign a number above 11, like in the broken leg example, the story needs to be trimmed into something more manageable.

At the end of the sizing process, each story will be assigned a number, aka, *story points*. Based on experience, an Engineering team may know they can complete a specific number of story points during a two-week development cycle, aka, a *sprint*. If a Product Manager is given the number of story points that will fit into the sprint, they will choose the most important combination of stories for the team to implement.

The goal of Scrum is for Engineering teams to deliver working software at a regular cadence. Limiting the duration of sprints helps ensure that stories aren't obsolete before engineers complete them. Moreover, short sprints enable the team to focus intensely on a manageable chunk of work during the sprint.

The best track and field sprinters have ample fast-twitch muscle fibers as opposed to the slow-twitch muscle fibers of endurance athletes. Sprinters go fast, empty their tanks, and then need to rest. An Agile sprint is similar—the team works heads-down, uninterrupted, to complete their stories in a short burst of speed. Then they rest up and regroup. Sprints are not marathons. After a sprint ends, Scrum teams have a *retrospective* where the team evaluates what went well, what didn't, and how to improve/pivot in the next sprint.

Kanban

Kanban is an Agile methodology focused on task visualization. Although Kanban supports all the *Agile Manifesto* principles, it lacks the structure and constraints of Scrum. The key to Kanban is a board that displays all the tasks that may be accomplished in a development cycle. When engineers select their tasks, a Kanban board provides a window into who is responsible for each piece of work. Typically, a Kanban board has several columns that reflect the various stages of completion—evaluation, in-progress, in-review, in-testing, and finished.

The concept of sprinting belongs to Scrum. Kanban is more of a marathon where engineers work steadily until all the work items are completed or when the due date arrives. Nothing in Kanban, however, precludes working in short bursts. This merging of Scrum and Kanban is called *Scrumban* and marries the structural and cultural advantages of Scrum with the visualization of Kanban.

Kanban work is governed by a concept called *Work In Progress (WIP)*. Each engineer is only permitted a limited amount of WIP and, therefore, cannot take on new work until enough preexisting work is completed.

Think of the beloved *I Love Lucy* episode when Lucy and Ethel worked in the chocolate factory. Their job was to wrap chocolates in paper as they came off the assembly line and place them back onto the conveyor belt. They were told that they'd be fired if any chocolates were unwrapped. Initially, the assembly line moved slowly. Lucy and Ethel kept up easily and smugly believed the job was a cinch. When their supervisor saw her two workers succeeding, she sped up the assembly line and left the room. Lucy and Ethel couldn't keep up—they stuffed chocolates in their mouths, in their hats, and in their blouses (Lucy and the Chocolate Factory, YouTube 2012).

The chocolate factory violated the WIP rule of Kanban. The results were compromised by pushing too much work onto the new employees. Lucy and Ethel ate more chocolate than they wrapped. The point of WIP is to govern work so that engineers can concentrate without becoming overwhelmed.

Extreme Programming

The previous two methodologies, Scrum and Kanban, are targeted at Software Development teams but are easily adaptable for any team that needs to produce reliable and transparent small-batch work. *Extreme Programming (XP)* is more technically focused than the other two and, therefore, harder to adapt to nonengineering pursuits.

Explaining a few of XP's key practices helps to illustrate the technical nature of this methodology:

Pair Programming is an XP key practice mandating two programmers work together to write or modify a piece of code. A manager might reasonably inquire, "If I'm paying big bucks for two programmers, why should they work on the same code instead of working separately and completing twice the number of features?"

XP aficionados explain that by working together, the product of two programmers' work is guaranteed to be more robust and better reasoned than one programmer's solution. This *two heads are better than one* approach ultimately saves money. By working out the technical kinks upfront, the pair programming-produced software doesn't require extensive code review nor is it likely to have bugs.

Test-Driven Development (TDD) is another XP key practice requiring programmers to write tests that assess the effectiveness of the feature before writing the code itself. If this sounds crazy, it's not. To write upfront tests of nonexistent code, a programmer must have a clear idea about the purpose of the code and how it will be used.

Continuous Integration/Continuous Delivery (CI/CD) is a third important XP key practice followed by many Engineering teams. Remember the *Agile Manifesto* principle that reads, "Working software over comprehensive documentation?" CI/CD provides Engineering teams with a way to deliver the working software. That is, CI/CD is a technical solution for putting software in front of customers.

The challenge of delivering working software to customers requires significantly more than a programmer applying their brilliance to the keyboard. After the code is completed, it must be deployed to a testing environment where automated tests and manual tests validate the work. The continuous integration part of CI/CD handles the deployment automation and commences automated tests. Following a green light from the Quality team, the continuous deployment part of CI/CD pushes the software into a production environment, so customers get their working software.

Implementing a CI/CD system is nontrivial and typically involves at least one dedicated employee. Most Development teams buy a CI/CD framework or use an open-source product instead of building this functionality in-house. Most frameworks require a scripting language to pull code from a source code repository and perform the builds. CI/CD needs additional scripting to invoke automated tests. The frameworks typically alert developers of test failures that demand their attention.

Lean Development

Lean development is a jaunty name for the manufacturing process, originated by Toyota in the mid-20th century, to streamline the production of cars and eliminate waste. Lean development takes its cues from these Toyota manufacturing principles (ProductPlan.com 2022):

1. **Value** to the customer—the streamlined approach is designed to deliver more functionality in less time.
2. **Value stream**—mapping every step that is required to bring functionality from conception to completion.
3. **Flow**—the consistent, immediate movement of work items through the value stream.
4. **Pull**—build products based on preorders rather than *Field of Dreams* thinking—*If we build it, they will come.*
5. **Perfection**—teams are self-managing and encouraged to seek continuous improvement.

Although the manufacturing process results in tangible goods, and software projects produce bits and bytes, the two have enough similarities to make Lean a viable development methodology. Much of the Lean Development methodology borrows heavily from the other methodologies, especially Scrum and XP. However, Lean development takes a more philosophical approach, focusing on waste reduction by under-engineering and building only on demand. The elimination of bottlenecks to create flow parallels Scrum's daily standup meetings, which are intended to identify blocker problems and nip them in the bud.

Lean development requires both a strong, disciplined team and comprehensive documentation. If either is lacking, Lean may not be the most appropriate methodology. On the other hand, for the right team in the right circumstances, Lean ruthlessly focuses on waste reduction and eliminates any activities that don't contribute directly to delivering the agreed-upon functionality.

A Few Final Words About Agile Methodologies

One of the guiding principles of the *Agile Manifesto* is that teams must be self-managing and take responsibility for their work. The autonomy afforded Development teams also applies to decision-making around

their development processes. Very few teams follow the textbook definition of any methodology to the letter. Instead, teams determine the best
approach for their unique situation. Managers overseeing multiple teams
may demand a single set of rules across the board, but this will be successful only if the multiple teams buy into the same rules.

Typically, large Engineering departments are separated into smaller
development teams. One team may choose to use Scrum and another
Kanban. A third may combine the two and use Scrumban. A fourth may
choose XP. Although these different approaches may rankle a microman-
ager, there's nothing wrong with teams choosing how they want to work
because a methodology has no effect on the final product. If a team meets
its goals, how they accomplish the feat is no one's business.*

*Two caveats:

1. Development teams are seldom static. Programmers may hop from
   team to team for many different reasons. If each team's methodology
   is different, there may be a small period of adjustment that's easily
   surmountable with a little extra effort.
2. Development teams don't exist in a vacuum. Large engineering groups
   are separated into teams for efficiency, but they must coordinate their
   schedules. Therefore, the duration of work iterations may require
   inter-team agreement, even if each group's methodologies differ.

In many respects, the four methodologies feel like the search to build
a better mousetrap. Except for XP, the other methodologies have core
similarities with slightly different implementation details.

Becoming wrapped up in the mechanics of a methodology to the
detriment of forward progress is verboten by the *Agile Manifesto* tenet,
"Individuals and interactions over processes and tools." So, *caveat emptor.*
Methodologies may prescribe rules and behaviors but should never get in
the way of delivering software.

Key Takeaways

1. The 2001 *Agile Manifesto* reflects a new way of thinking, mostly
   replacing the older Waterfall approach to software development.
2. The *Agile Manifesto* is a philosophy of software development that
   espouses a pragmatic small-batch approach to delivering working

software. Overall, the Agile Manifesto's importance is favoring communication and collaboration with fellow programmers and customers over an onerous cycle of documentation and written specifications.

3. The biggest problem with the Waterfall method is the design phase takes so long that the business problem will change before the design is completed.

4. There are some valuable aspects of a Waterfall approach like gaining a holistic understanding of a product domain, sometimes lost with the uptake of Agile.

5. The Agile Manifesto is written in simple English but is often misunderstood. The *Agile Manifesto* recommends balancing process with communication, not eliminating process.

6. An Agile methodology industry was formed to address the difficulty of successfully implementing Agile.

7. The most popular Agile methodology, Scrum, recommends short cycles of work called sprints, in which programmers complete work contained in user stories describing the *what* and *why* of a problem.

8. XP is the most technical of the Agile methodologies, introducing concepts like pair programming, TDD, and CI/CD.

9. Each methodology has strengths and weaknesses. Most programming teams that adopt a methodology never follow it completely. Instead, teams tend to take the pieces that fit into their workstyle and improvise.

10. Ultimately, implementing a methodology for Agile is more important than the specific methodology that's chosen.

CHAPTER 3

Holistic Challenges of Agile

While originally intended for software development, the sensible ideas in the *Agile Manifesto* apply equally to Marketing, Sales, HR, and all other departments in a company. The challenge for non-Engineering groups is taking an idea like, "Working software over comprehensive documentation," and making it meaningful for the non-technical tasks at hand.

Agile methodologies, like XP, focus on the technical nitty-gritty and have no crossover application for nontechnical usage. The more general Scrum methodology, however, is usage-agnostic. Granted, the originators of Scrum and the other Agile methodologies had software delivery in mind just as the *Agile Manifesto* guys sought innovative ways to better approach software projects.

The following case study explores the application of an Agile methodology and the *Agile Manifesto* philosophy to an entirely non technical business problem. Anyone in a growing company will be familiar with this use case. The challenge of hiring stellar candidates can overwhelm even moderate-sized HR teams. However, an Agile approach to the problem yields surprising results.

Case Study: Growing a Company

A software startup receives a large angel investment, enabling it to expand its team. The newly appointed Director of HR, Nisha, is tasked with creating and executing a hiring plan, thus enabling the company to make good on its ambitious promises to dominate its market.

A tall order, indeed, for a recent psychology major without any hiring experience. Nisha fell into her job responsibilities because she successfully arbitrated a scuffle over the last Pamplemousse La Croix seltzer water that two developers simultaneously grabbed for in the kitchen. Since she exhibited more maturity than the developers, it was decided she possessed the necessary people skills to scale up the company. Plus, the CEO had previously witnessed Nisha's emotional intelligence and recognized he had no one else on staff to do the job.

Bright employees working in startups may end up in positions they never imagined because of an urgent corporate need. Startups have rich histories of giving inexperienced employees challenging positions where they sink or swim. This new head of HR is determined to swim.

Initial Waterfall Plans

Nisha's first instinct is to demonstrate her mastery of scaling the organization by concocting a six-month plan that results in filling all the open positions. Sure, it will take hard work, but Nisha reasons she can sleep when she retires. She imagines she'll gain the respect of her manager and peers if she consistently logs 80-hour weeks and fills open positions through sheer grit and determination.

Nisha's mentor, the VP of Engineering, Jamal, makes a few gentle suggestions. At first, Nisha is reluctant to listen to her 45-year-old mentor. The other Gen-Zers consider Jamal the office grandpa. Instead of engaging in Nerf gun wars or Foosball tournaments in the office, Jamal spends his day huddled with the Engineering team around the whiteboard in his office. Instead of hitting the bars with his coworkers after they knock off at 10:00 pm, Jamal leaves hours before anyone else to have dinner with his family and put his children to bed. Jamal's rep around the office is that he neither works hard nor plays hard.

The 25-year-old CEO, however, absolutely loves Jamal. Maybe that's because the Engineering team consistently meets or exceeds its goals and never misses a deliverable. For all the crazy hours logged by the other departments, none of them comes anywhere close to Engineering's performance.

Some Agile Advice

So, Nisha decides to listen to whatever Jamal has to say. Jamal makes the following general points:

1. You don't understand this company's mission well enough to understand its hiring needs. You shouldn't confuse your title with actual experience. Block out time to develop expertise in what you're undertaking.

2. If you make a six-month plan, there are too many unknowns that will interfere with your ultimate goals. Making a grandiose plan with a big payoff at the end is like a Vegas high roller who bets his entire savings on one spin of the roulette wheel. You need to accumulate smaller wins instead of making one huge bet that you're likely to lose.

3. Break this big hiring problem into smaller, accomplishable chunks. Make sure you can measure success or failure for each smaller piece of work. Set yourself up for success by committing to reasonably difficult but achievable goals.

4. Don't be timid. Take some educated risks and stretch yourself. However, if you break up the work into small pieces and fail, acknowledge the failures, take your lumps, and change course.

5. Figure out how to engage others in the plan because you cannot succeed at this alone. Remember that when you bring in others, they will have their own ideas that may differ from yours. Rather than viewing opposing ideas as a challenge to your authority, figure out how to incorporate the best ideas to make an even better plan.

Nisha listens politely to Jamal. Not once does he mention the 80-hour workweeks Nisha was planning nor does he imply that success will only come from Nisha's heroism and sacrifice. Instead, Jamal is suggesting an entirely different approach that almost guarantees success without punishing hours. Nisha finally understands the business cliché, *work smarter, not harder.*

As Nisha reviews her notes, Jamal's first point about her lack of company knowledge stings as much as it did when he uttered it. Still, Nisha is fearful of the daunting task ahead of her and believes that Jamal is correct. Engaging in a period of deep learning is better than a *fake it until you make it* approach.

Biting Off a Small Chunk of Work

Nisha already has managers from Marketing, Engineering, Product, and Sales knocking on her cubicle wall. The four managers are each making their pitches to get the largest piece of the hiring pie. She decides to start with a two-week directed learning project. The goal of this project is to understand the overall business plan and to understand the expected contribution of each team. By speaking to the team leaders, digging into financials, and understanding business plans, Nisha hopes to better understand the skill-set gaps of the current teams. Although she expects to learn there are more needs than her pot of money will cover, her goal is to understand the relative importance of each team's objectives to meeting overall company goals.

Making It Measurable

Remembering Jamal's advice to make each block of work measurable, Nisha struggles to associate a metric with her two-week research effort. Watching *Shark Tank* one evening, Nisha discovers her metric. She will present her research findings, opinions, and conclusions to the executive team. If she emerges with only a few nibbles from the sharks, she'll know that she's on the right track. If she's eaten alive, it's back to the drawing board.

At the end of the two-week effort, Nisha presents her findings to the Management team. Referring to the period as her firehose of education, the HR Director explains her surprising conclusions. Instead of finding that one group's needs exceeded another group's needs, she observed a delicate interdependence between the groups. Nisha tries to sell the idea that hiring should be proportionally spread through the different teams in the company.

The CEO is the first to take a bite out of Nisha. He wants to spend the bulk of the investment money to double the Engineering team. He reasons that the capacity problems Jamal's team faces will be solved by adding bodies. Nisha isn't surprised by the CEO's reaction. He founded the company and was its first developer. The belief that adding bodies to the Engineering team will solve all of a company's problems is endemic of technical CEOs.

Nisha is prepared. She counters that chaos will ensue if the Engineering team grows disproportionately to the Product Management team. The newly hired engineers' heightened need for solid specifications will exceed Product Management's capacity. Similarly, if the Product and Engineering teams grow, their increased output will require additional salespeople and marketers. She devised a formula to produce a general headcount plan by division, based on the relative sizes of the present groups and the available budget.

The CEO grouses a bit. When Jamal and the other leaders back up Nisha, the CEO admits he doesn't have all the answers, which is why he relies on his smart executive team. He then points out that what he envisioned as a hiring effort confined to one department is now a larger endeavor spread out through the entire company. He wants to ensure fairness in hiring across departments, hiring for cultural fit, and the technical expertise of every candidate as it relates to their position. In short, the CEO challenges Nisha to put together a holistic hiring plan that works for each department.

Building a Self-Managing Team

Remembering Jamal's last piece of advice about engaging other people in her cause, Nisha uses the Management team's support to corral them into becoming members of her Hiring team. She devises another two-week effort to create a plan to address all of the CEO's concerns. Initially, Nisha intended to ask each department head to produce the draft requirements for their open positions. She planned to use the drafts to write polished, cohesive position descriptions.

When she assembles a kickoff meeting, her new team has different ideas. As the most experienced and successful Hiring Manager, Jamal takes the lead. He shocks everyone by recommending scrapping traditional interviews. He claims that most people lie during job interviews, which often results in hiring the best actor. Instead, he advocates using an hour to audition candidates, giving them problems to assess their creative, analytical, technical, and strategic capabilities. For engineers, Jamal's team will sit with candidates working together on a few carefully selected programming problems designed to expose the aforementioned capabilities. Jamal explains that the process of collaborating to solve problems also reveals a candidate's willingness to lead, willingness to take direction, and provides a window into their inherent curiosity.

Jamal barely finishes speaking when the other department heads start excitedly imagining how they will audition candidates in a similar manner. As a group, the managers agree to provide Nisha with the basic requirements for their job positions and let her craft them into compelling position descriptions. They also commit to each other to have their audition scripts ready by the end of the two-week period.

At first, Nisha is miffed that Jamal stepped in and derailed her plan. When she sees the enthusiasm from her colleagues, she remembers Jamal's point that the best ideas emerge from an empowered team. She riffs on Jamal's idea, suggesting she first engage candidates in a short behavioral interview to assess cultural fit, discuss salary expectations, and explain the logistics of the interview process. She also suggests incorporating a final executive interview to field candidate questions and explain company strategic direction. She gets buy-in from the team.

Nisha feels less like a one-woman band and more like the quarterback of a championship team.

Evaluation of the HR Case Study

The HR case study stops before the hiring process is completed because its point is to illustrate how to apply Agile principles to an untraditional situation. Rest assured, Nisha and her team continue their short work cycles and hire many superstars.

The most important Agile aspect of Nisha's approach is the decomposition of the big problem of hiring lots of new employees into smaller, more manageable problems. Without knowing any Agile terminology, Nisha took Jamal's advice and planned sprints. Each sprint ended with a completed, measurable deliverable. If any aspect of the sprint failed and they needed to change course, the team would lose no more than the two-week work effort. If Nisha hadn't listened to Jamal and embarked on her six-month Waterfall project, failure at the end would be catastrophic.

Nisha also set aside time for learning. Remember, she went into the hiring project as a new hire herself, fresh out of college with absolutely no people management experience. Injecting some Agile terminology, Nisha created a *research spike* that is sprint time devoted to studying and learning. Agile teams must frequently tackle new things. Time-boxing the learning into a short sprint keeps the research directed and avoids a sustained academic project.

Nisha's self-managing team is another important Agile concept. One of the key pillars of the *Agile Manifesto* is the trust in teams to take responsibility for their work product. In her case, Nisha recruited her Hiring Team, giving them enough freedom to be innovative and flesh out an untraditional hiring approach.

At first, Nisha equated the creation of a self-managing team with the elimination of her management job. After all, if the team manages itself, they don't need a manager. Nisha discovered, however, that even if the team didn't need a people manager, there was a lot of process to manage. She provided much-needed oversight to ensure the hiring process was fair within each department and equitable across the company.

The HR Director created an Agile process with Jamal's guidance without knowing the first thing about Agile.

Why Extend Agile Beyond Software Teams?

Yes, a bunch of software people invented the Agile Manifesto, and they intended for it to help them solve frustrating and thorny software development problems. However, it's easy to substitute a couple of words in the *Agile Manifesto* and its underlying principles, like *software* and *developers*, to make it applicable to all of a company's departments.

A contrarian might argue that generalizing something as specific as the *Agile Manifesto* invariably results in a half-baked philosophy that doesn't really apply to anything. The counterargument is that the *Agile Manifesto* is a *philosophy*, and philosophies are typically nonspecific. The *methodologies* like Lean, Scrum, and XP are software-specific, and some aspects may not be adaptable to non technical work products. If a methodology doesn't fit the use case, it's the wrong methodology, and it's necessary to either find a new methodology or cook up a new one.

Measuring Progress

Look beneath the glossy veneer of any company and imperfections emerge. Understanding these imperfections is one of the most challenging aspects of a CEO's job. Suppose Sales isn't hitting their goals and points the finger at Engineering, saying they're not delivering sellable software. Passing the buck, Engineering throws Product Management under the bus, by insisting that their requirements are wrong. Without a transparent process for measuring across-the-board success or failure, otherwise functional companies often resort to political finger-pointing to avoid accepting responsibility.

Truthfully, when Sales misses their targets, it's almost impossible to unwind the cause without having measurements attached to each team's deliverables. Even then, missing a sales goal can indicate a host of underlying problems. Sometimes missing a sales goal is just a bad twist of fate where the high probability prospects in a Sales pipeline inexplicably dry up. Missing sales goals may occur for a multitude of reasons.

Generally, latching onto trends is preferable to reacting to individual data points. If a Sales team consistently misses its targets, perhaps it is aiming too high, the company's product is uncompetitive, or the salespeople aren't trying hard enough.

Rather than guessing at the problem, evaluating each team on empirical criteria helps to identify problem areas. For example, suppose each team commits to objectives like these:

1. **Sales**—Quarterly, each salesperson will develop five new prospects, work with a sales engineer to give five data demos, and close U.S.$100K in new sales.
2. **Product Management**—Quarterly, each Product team will fully explore the next quarter's roadmap items in enough detail to make go/no-go decisions. For the items that are deemed worth developing, Product Management will produce a full set of market analysis, feature sets, and collateral information like mockups and prototypes.
3. **Engineering**—The Engineering team will make weekly production deployments that iteratively deliver the feature sets specified by Product Management. By the end of the quarter, each feature set defined by Product Management will be completed as agreed upon by the teams and delivered to customers.

Although these objectives are broad and somewhat vague, if Engineering and Product Management deliver as promised and Sales still misses its goals, it helps identify the problem's nexus.

The most significant challenge with objectives is making them empirically testable. It takes effort and know-how to craft objectives for scientific measurement. For example, take Nisha's first goal in her HR project to better understand the business. Instead of making learning the goal of the research spike and determining success or failure by how much the Management team chews her up, Nisha would do better to state what she intends to learn and be judged on the success or failure of concrete objectives. If Nisha had specified the following goals for her learning spike, it would be easy to evaluate her success:

1. State the three most significant product features that are in jeopardy this quarter because of capacity issues.
2. Of these three features in jeopardy, state the profitability of each given the company meets its quarterly sales forecast.
3. Identify the prospective customers who are most likely to be influenced to buy because of these features. Explain the problems these customers are attempting to solve and how the features are essential.
4. Present three different departmental headcounts and explain how each contributes to the success of the company's goals.

Failing Fast

Failing fast is one of the most overworked business tropes. The underlying motivation is for companies to take big risks with immense potential payoffs. To fail fast, the company must put sensors in place to recognize early if the risky move is panning out and worth continuing.

In comparative mythology, the hero's journey requires the protagonist to face and overcome adversity before they become worthy of winning. Biographers of business titans use the hero's journey construct to explain the role of failures in their ultimate successes.

It's one thing for Bill Gates to bemoan his reviled Clippy Office Assistant, which debuted in Microsoft Office 97. Everyone else who hasn't achieved Gates' level of success should be wary of highlighting their own failures.

In general, interviewers want to hear about the lessons candidates learn from failures. Candidates who glean especially insightful lessons may paint a positive picture of the failure. Ideally, fast failures are preferable to long failures, but time is relative. In some business scenarios, a one-year failure is considered short-term, while a three-month failure is considered long-term in another company.

Most prospective employees are savvy enough not to brag about their littered highways of failures during job interviews. Although a perceptive interviewer may want to dig into a candidate's failures to discover what they learned from the experience, this is red-flag territory, regardless of the beautiful credo of failing fast.

Most corporate failures occur excruciatingly slowly, like watching a tomato seed sprout without time-lapse photography. Companies with a Waterfall mentality may initially scrutinize a nascent idea with a gimlet eye, but green light it based on a projected profitability assessment. The problem with Waterfall is its lack of mid-cycle milestones to recognize possible cost overruns, unforeseen development complications, or an altered business landscape that changes the idea's profitability calculus. Since the completed product isn't delivered until the very end of a Waterfall project, failure awaits the final evaluation.

The ethos of Agile sprints is that they are discrete. A team may elect to follow one sprint with a second sprint to continue the work, but this is a conscious decision and not a *fait accompli*. Sometimes a Development team encounters unforeseen complications that slow their sprint progress. Before electing to continue the work in a follow-on sprint, Product Management will revise its estimates for the completion date of the feature. The cost or time overrun may render the feature unviable, and it's killed or shelved after the first failed sprint.

There's no shame in failure when it's recognized after one or two sprints. Low-cost failures are easy to sweep under the carpet. Realistically, however, recognizing true failure takes longer than one or two sprints.

A sunk cost mentality frequently overtakes reason in Waterfall's slow failures. Managers reason that they've already invested so much it's best to keep pouring money into the feature. Buying one's way out of failure is an expensive proposition that compounds the problem.

Accountability

Agile teams are self-managing, which means they mostly call their own shots. Product Management typically determines what an Agile team should build, but deciding how to accomplish the tasks is up to the team.

Professionals will gladly accept accountability if they're free to control their destinies. If things go south in a sprint, self-managing teams accept the failure, dust themselves off, and devise a better approach should the stakeholders decide to continue the work.

The managers banded together in Nisha's HR team to espouse an alternative to traditional candidate interviewing. Each manager defined the *audition* script for their positions to expose candidates' creative, analytical, technical, and strategic capabilities. If the process failed to provide a window into the important candidate qualities, each manager should tweak the audition script. After all, no one outside the team imposed this approach—the innovation came from within. Therefore, the responsibility rests with the team.

Overcoming Across-the-Board Agile Challenges

When a CEO brags, "We're an Agile company," they imply the company turns on a dime, immediately responding to the vicissitudes of the business landscape. In most companies, Agile is limited to Engineering teams that use some manner of Agile methodology. The disconnect between a CEO's imagination and operational reality is resolvable by having leaders across the company read and absorb the *Agile Manifesto*. By challenging each leader to craft Agile for their respective departments, an ambitious CEO might ultimately transform their lumbering company into an Agile company.

Leadership Is Required to Adopt Agile

The HR case study illustrates Nisha's process to craft Agile principles for her HR domain. Nisha was wise to listen to her mentor, Jamal, who was already running an Agile Engineering team. A catalyst like Jamal is sometimes sufficient to pique colleagues' imaginations in underperforming divisions. However, across-the-board agility usually requires a top-down push from the CEO. A department that radically changes its workstyle faces significant risks. A CEO endorsing small-batch work and constant reflection and reevaluation provides the space for departments to take risks.

Is Agile for the Long Game?

Senior leaders may push back when asked to radically change their approach. A VP of Sales, for example, might argue that Agile doesn't apply to them because they're playing the long game. The enterprise software sales process is usually slow, based on cultivating relationships, reaching the people who make purchasing decisions, and convincing them to find space in a future budget. Great salespeople keep the flame lit even when the prospective customer focuses on other higher priorities. The CEO might counter that the yearly forecast from sales is always incorrect, sometimes disastrously incorrect. By adopting Agile principles, the VP of Sales can fine-tune forecasts, respond to changes, and help salespeople manage their workloads in small batches.

Where Does Agile Fall Short?

Mistakes will occur in adapting a philosophy intended for software development to the other departments of a company. Since there are no rules or established methodologies for nonsoftware development Agility, HR, Sales, Product Management, Marketing, and Finance are trailblazers. Some trial and error is to be expected.

These are two red flags for managers to recognize and avoid:

1. *Process heaviness* is more a methodology problem than an Agile philosophical problem. For example, if the Marketing team wastes time every morning with a daily standup meeting, cadged from Scrum, this may not be the right kind of meeting to have if the team's work is largely noncollaborative. Instead, it might be more beneficial to focus discussions on handoff points from one team member to another, and forgo daily meetings.
2. *Excluding the big picture* is a misunderstanding of Agile philosophy. In most cases, it's counterproductive to make concrete plans far into the future. Agilists may mistakenly focus only on the immediate with no regard for the future. For example, if HR plans an ambitious rework of company policies, complete with benefits changes, it's a long-term project requiring several milestones. Focusing exclusively on writing a new employee manual without planning to interview new insurance companies is too myopic.

Key Takeaways

1. The *Agile Manifesto* was written by Software Developers attempting to codify a better software development process.
2. Regardless of the originator's intentions, the *Agile Manifesto* is a philosophy easily adaptable to a company's non-Engineering functions.
3. The most important aspect of Agile is chunking work into smaller pieces, each of which can be completed quickly.
4. With practice and guidance, any short-term deliverable may be defined to be empirically measurable.
5. Biting off small pieces of a large project and addressing them in short sprints promotes the concept of failing fast. If an idea doesn't pan out in a two-week sprint, there's not enough sunk cost to cause pain or prevent a change in direction.
6. Self-managing teams bring innovation and accountability to projects.
7. Establishing across-the-board agility requires the buy-in from the most senior management.
8. Senior employees may push back when asked to transition from a Waterfall mentality to an Agile mentality.
9. Process heaviness is one of the ways a project can get bogged down. Teams can avoid the quicksand of too much process by focusing less on Agile methodologies and more on the principles of Agile.
10. There's no playbook for across-the-board Agile. Smart, thoughtful leaders will work with their teams to devise processes that fit their needs.

CHAPTER 4

The Dirty Secret of Agile

Ask just about any technical team nowadays and they'll claim they're using some flavor of Agile practices in lieu of the debunked Waterfall method. Teams using Scrum may engage in *story point poker-playing*, a method of estimating the level of effort of stories. Or they may actually relinquish their chairs for daily standup meetings. The corniness of Scrum aside, there's no arguing that the *Agile Manifesto* is rock solid. Still, the technical landscape is dotted with software releases that don't cut the mustard, from quality problems to software that fails to effectively address customers' most significant pain points.

Perhaps the most important tenet of the *Agile Manifesto* is to build working software one piece at a time. If a team adheres to the Scrum methodology, they work heads-down in short sprints writing software and attempting to finish it by the end of the work cycle. The only way to build something functional after a short work period is to be certain of the requirements before beginning. With Scrum, certainty comes from well-considered and right-sized user stories that enable developers to work without digging for answers to fundamental questions.

The concept of heads-down sprinting applies equally to any other department undertaking an Agile approach to their work. Before beginning a sprint, the people on the team must possess a deep understanding of the problems being addressed, how to finish the stories, and the parameters that define success.

Practical Challenge of Agile #1: Research Spikes

What if a team is attempting something they've never undertaken and need to learn before they can effectively tackle the work? The *Agile Manifesto* isn't much help here, but the purpose of philosophy isn't to fill in all the nitty-gritty details. The Agile *methodologies* exist to help address some of the practical details. Scrum provides the concept of a *Research Spike* to block time for learning within the confines of a sprint. Like other user stories, a research spike is a time-boxed iteration of work. Unlike other user stories, research spikes do not result in working software—they result in learning.

In the HR example in Chapter 3, Nisha devotes an entire two-week sprint to learning about the business. Her goal isn't to get a quickie MBA. Instead, Nisha hopes to learn just enough to develop an educated opinion about how to best structure her company's recruitment program.

Research spikes are a pragmatic addition to Scrum utilized by most teams in the normal course of tackling new projects.

Practical Challenge of Agile #2: Continuity

Figure 4.1 depicts the typical Agile Scrum work cycle. The portion to the left of the Scrum team circle concerns sprint planning. Typically, a Product Manager reviews the *backlog,* a collection of already-written user stories, and determines the best ones to tackle in the upcoming sprint. Before starting the sprint, the developers meet with the Product Manager to seek clarification about the stories. After the meeting ends, the sprint begins, and the clock starts ticking. The development team works heads-down, hopefully avoiding distractions until the sprint ends. The software is delivered at the end of the sprint, and the team slows down to reflect on the good, the bad, and the ugly of the previous sprint, vowing to do better next time. Then the process starts all over again.

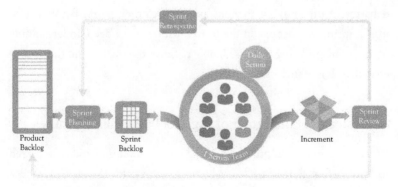

Figure 4.1 Scrum framework

Source: Scrum Framework ©2020 Scrum.org.

The Hidden Implications of a Product Backlog

On paper, the workflow of Scrum sprints appears orderly and well considered. A sprint planning meeting is considered successful if the Product Manager answers all the developers' questions. However, large, complicated projects of any type require a depth of thought that isn't represented in the diagram. Implicit in the product backlog, the repository of user stories, is a full and thorough discovery process that precedes a sprint planning meeting.

User Stories are intentionally vague because they're intended to prompt enough discussion to fill in the missing gaps. Often, the missing gaps are large enough to necessitate creating additional stories. The sprint planning meetings with the development team, typically no more than a couple of hours, are long enough for developers to poke holes in stories and receive guidance. Sprint planning meetings, however, are too short to fully explore the contours of each user story.

A vital part of the process for delivering stellar work products is scheduling in-depth discussions and taking the time to let ideas gel before writing the first user story.

For any application of Agile across a company, it's important to remember there are no shortcuts in problem-solving. The hard work of understanding the core nugget of a problem and building a solution to address it elegantly and sensibly isn't any easier with Agile. Sometimes, an Agile approach obfuscates the true problems with too-vague stories that are inadequately explored.

Scenario: Zoom-Like Communications App

Suppose an Engineering team is asked to build a Zoom-like product supporting audio and video calls. The Product Management team would likely break the problem into manageable chunks, perhaps focusing first on person-to-person audio calls.

Almost everyone has experience making phone calls and using Zoom, GoTo-Meeting, or Slack. The hidden risk in undertaking seemingly familiar problem domains, like audio calls, is the hubris of assuming known problems are simple and don't require deep analysis.

If a Product Manager spends an afternoon thinking about the app and reviewing competitors' products, writing a large set of user stories for all the features an audio call app requires is simple. This Product Manager may believe they have met their responsibility after holding a two-hour planning meeting with the Engineering team to clarify and fine-tune the user stories. Unfortunately, a Product Manager who acts alone to frame a feature set is working in a vacuum. Feature discovery is a collaborative act demanding interaction with stakeholders.

Examples of How a Sprint Fails

The Engineering team is confident they understand the requirements to build the person-to-person audio app. The Product Manager has whittled the list of must-have features down to a set the engineers believe they can accomplish in their first two-week sprint. They begin and the clock starts ticking.

The first obstacle the team faces is technical, creating the back-end for a notification server. The notification server is responsible for alerting users to incoming calls. Although the team knew they would need to spend time building this back-end service, the Product Manager neglected to write these targeted stories. Instead, stories like, "As a user, I want to be notified when a call comes in because I may be using another application on my phone and otherwise wouldn't see the call come in," imply that a notification service is required. However, there are no stories that delve into the specifications and performance requirements of the notification service. Therefore, the team needs to stop and work with Product Management to produce specifications for the notification server.

The second obstacle reflects insufficient discussion. In this case, the Product Manager focuses on how users receive text notifications on their phones to the exclusion of other scenarios. Everyone has experienced missing an incoming call because they're away from their phone. Phones offer a rich set of ringtones to provide audio notifications. Yet, the sprint starts without any stories about the phone ringing to announce incoming calls. Additionally, the call's initiator should hear a tone when the phone is dialing. Although it's not a huge technical challenge to make a phone ring or provide a dial tone, inserting missed user stories in an already full story bucket is the sort of scope creep that immutable sprints should prevent.

Merits of Waterfall

One benefit of Waterfall is that its exhaustive upfront exploration would likely prevent both of the two aforementioned sprint failures. The notification server would be explicitly identified and scoped in a Waterfall process, along with the details of every other piece of the application. The detailed workflows in a Waterfall project would have also uncovered the requirement for audio notifications of incoming calls.

The key merit of Waterfall is that *nothing* falls through the cracks.

Weaknesses of Waterfall

The inadvisability of planning out an entire system upfront is already addressed in earlier chapters and needn't be reiterated. The lack of technical diversity among the team is an infrequently discussed but equally damaging aspect of Waterfall. The team performing the lengthy upfront analysis and design typically comprises product managers and designers. Although a Waterfall team may identify the technical pieces and specify the requirements, they will probably not have the technical chops to evaluate the approach's feasibility.

Many engineers say, "From a technical perspective, almost anything is possible." However, the subtext of their statement is, "Anything is possible provided you're willing to pay exorbitant sums and wait forever." Product Management's role is to understand any feature's potential return on investment (ROI). ROI is roughly calculated by estimating the sales boost and subtracting development costs. Technically complex solutions are sometimes infeasible from an ROI perspective. Waterfall's fatal flaw is omitting engineers capable of assessing technical difficulties from the upfront design team.

Multidisciplinary Exploration Teams

The cycle of planning, sprinting, retrospectives, and recalibrating doesn't leave much space to tackle complexity. Even the simplest-sounding endeavors mask complexity under a thin veneer. Once a team looks under the hood at a seemingly easy problem, they will undoubtedly discover challenges they hadn't even contemplated.

Examples of the myth of simplicity could easily fill an entire book. Take any endeavor like operating a soft-serve ice cream shop and it will have its unique issues that a layperson would never imagine. The same holds true for the problems spanning the different departments in a company. Nothing is ever as simple as it appears from the outside.

In an earlier case study, the HR manager, Nisha, spent a couple of weeks learning. Her learning time was considered a research spike as part of a sprint. Sometimes, however, it isn't possible to time-box the learning and evaluation process. Before a company commits to any new, significant project, prudent managers attempt to first understand the value of the project. Most smart managers will reject a project if it is so difficult and time-consuming that it's unlikely to ever pay for itself. Discovering whether a project is or isn't worth the effort is a devilishly difficult determination that usually requires more than a two-week research spike.

One challenge of ROI determination is entirely distinct from the technical aspects of project completion. Estimating customer demand and determining the optimal price point of a new product or feature set are often as difficult as providing a solution.

A business exploration team behaves much like a military reconnaissance scout, surreptitiously spying on the enemy's position before committing an entire unit to annihilation. Fortunately, it's not life or death in a business setting, but the business exploration team can save the larger team from costly mistakes that might potentially kill a company.

The goals of an exploration team are to make a learned-enough feasibility judgment and to gain some general ideas about how best to approach the problem. If the exploration team develops expertise and fully designs a solution, they have likely veered into a Waterfall approach and need to rein themselves in.

Exploration Team Model for the Audio App

In the previous scenario where an engineering team is asked to build an audio app for person-to-person calls, they embark on the work only to discover hidden landmines that scuttle the sprint. Exploration teams evaluate approaches to the work without producing a design specification. Although the exploration team's work is open-ended without the constraint of a short sprint, the team members are sensitive to the balance between making informed decisions and getting a product to market. That is, the exploration team performs directed research, not a PhD dissertation.

In much the same way, engineers in a sprint planning meeting attempt to tease the underlying work from user stories, the exploration team seeks out the rough edges of a new project and works to understand them well enough to smooth them out. In the audio app example, the team may undertake these steps:

1. Design workflows for phone calls from the caller's and the call recipient's perspectives. The workflows should consider the different states of the recipient—receiving a call while using the app, receiving a call while using another app, receiving a call while away from the device, and receiving a call while the user is asleep.
2. Write brief narratives of the caller's and recipient's experiences in the different scenarios from #1.
3. Understand the delta between the backend technology required for calls and the software the engineering team has already developed.
4. Based on a set of performance specifications, assess the effort required to build the backend technology that doesn't already exist.
5. Research alternatives to building new software, like buying off-the-shelf backend software.
6. Evaluate the feasibility of building new software versus buying off-the-shelf software, and make recommendations.

An Exploration Dream Team

The audio app exploration team covers a lot of ground. Not only do they map the workflows, but they also research the build versus buy conundrum and assess the feasibility of building the backend in-house. The exploration team needs members with the skills to felicitously address each of the steps above. This discovery team requires the following roles:

1. Engineering—Assessing the feasibility of a technical solution demands an engineer with enough experience to be a credible source of information.
2. Design—This discovery exercise aims to understand the problem and explore potential approaches. Designers help the team and stakeholders to visualize the flow. The designer isn't attempting to provide high-fidelity renderings.
3. Quality—The quality team exists not just to test, but to assess the viability of proposed solutions from user experience and maintenance perspectives. Sometimes a nice user experience may be devilishly difficult to maintain.
4. Operations—The ability to deliver and deploy the software product is a key part of its feasibility. A proposed solution that demands an esoteric deployment package may be deemed too expensive and, therefore, infeasible.
5. Product—The Product Management role possesses the business understanding, user relationships, and market knowledge to assess the fit of the proposed solution.

The makeup of the team depends on the specifics of the exploration. If, for example, the exploration team is determining the best place to dig a mine, the team might consist of geologists, hydrologists, safety inspectors, and conservationists. The team to explore a new sales strategy might include Sales, Marketing, Finance, and Business Development.

A Common Denominator of Exploration Teams

Regardless of the exploration, the teams performing the discovery require a base of experience. Although the exploration team members don't have to possess precise knowledge of the topic, they should draw from a reservoir of varied knowledge. If the team has already performed the work they're exploring, there is no need to explore. The common denominator of all exploration teams is experience. The team members must have sufficient seniority to make relatively fast assessments without having all the facts.

Challenges of Assembling Exploration Teams

Bringing together a group of senior-level employees for an indeterminate amount of time poses two significant problems:

1. Employees with enough seniority to act as discovery trailblazers are valuable. Exploration isn't directly tied to profits, so the siren song of revenue may coerce management to give exploration the short shrift by delegating these senior employees to profit-generating activities. For example, a senior engineer capable of exploration is also an invaluable resource on Sales calls.
2. Roles on the exploration team are investigative, not executive. That is, the explorers get so close to executing a solution they can taste it, but they are intentional about not crossing the line. The explorer role may be frustrating for employees who derive satisfaction from building new things.

Mitigating Exploration Team Challenges

Software development teams are considered a cost center, yet these teams are considered a very expensive necessity. The folly of having an inadequately prepared development team embark on a sprint destined for failure should chagrin a company's bean counters. By framing exploration teams as the inoculation against wasted engineering sprints, it follows that exploration teams are as necessary as software teams.

Rather than yanking senior employees off other projects to perform discovery, budgeting for and building permanent teams demonstrates a commitment to this discipline. Building a permanent discovery team also ensures that the team members want to be there. The trailblazer role uniquely appeals to many, but it's not for everyone.

Putting It All Together—Case Study

StaidCorp is a fictitious life insurance company founded in 1920 by Hiram Staid. The company prospered through the 20th century selling term- and whole-life insurance policies. The StaidCorp business model included word-of-mouth sales with a strong agent network, magazine advertising, and direct mail campaigns. Management of StaidCorp passed from Hiram to his son, Hiram Staid II, in the 1970s. Hiram II's daughter Helene Staid has recently assumed control and envisions big changes to reinvigorate the company. Helene represents the third generation of Staids to steer the company.

Helene, a millennial, acknowledges that the StaidCorp sales model enabled the company to thrive for nearly a century, but this same sales model is now causing the company to flounder. Policyholders are dying faster than new ones are signing up.

As Helene explains to her father:

1. Word of mouth now occurs in online forums like Twitter (now X) or Signal.
2. Few pay attention to print advertisements.
3. Most people regard direct mail as junk that goes directly into the recycling bin.

Helene wants to digitize the primarily analog StaidCorp.

Helene is so certain she's correct about digitizing StaidCorp that she's willing to bet the company by restructuring and hiring a new crop of forward-thinking employees. The StaidCorp board, mainly consisting of old schoolers, doesn't doubt Helene's contentions but demands some empirical proof that it's the best direction to take the company.

The StaidCorp board is, in effect, demanding an exploration team scout the landscape and report on their reconnaissance before committing the entire company to potential bloodshed. Although Helene believes the exploration team will delay progress and ultimately corroborate what she already believes, she has no choice but to listen to the board.

Helene assembles an exploration team from senior staff who understand the ins and outs of the insurance business. Although StaidCorp has an old-school business model, it's a savvy insurance company with an analytics team run by PhD data scientists. Helene includes a senior data scientist on the exploration team. StaidCorp is thin on social media expertise, so Helene is forced to add a couple of college-aged interns.

Hiram Staid was an innovator in the life insurance industry. He intuited that people buy life insurance when they experience significant life milestones like marriage, buying a first house, childbirth, and death.

StaidCorp became notorious for stalking maternity ward halls to sign up new customers among the sleep-deprived, stressed fathers in the waiting rooms. Yes, these were sexist times when men were excluded from the birthing process. Even more egregiously, StaidCorp representatives attended funerals to sell insurance to children of deceased parents who were likely considering their own mortality.

Helene expects to retrofit Hiram Staid's arguably underhanded methods to the digital age. Rather than take advantage of people's vulnerability, Helene hopes to provide important insurance coverage when potential customers face life changes. She envisions microtargeting Facebook users, giving offers to people who post baby pictures. She hopes to use popup Google Ads to offer policies to people searching for a mortuary.

The exploration team poses several questions:

1. Will Hiram Staid's methods work in the digital age?
2. Is it possible to target potential customers based on what they post on Facebook, Twitter (now X), or Instagram?
3. Are there other digital approaches, like webinars and downloadable whitepapers, that will establish StaidCorp as thought leaders and draw in new customers?
4. Do millennials care about purchasing life insurance?
5. Will potential customers be turned off if they feel their privacy is being violated to sell them insurance?
6. How are competitors using the Web to sell insurance?
7. How can we determine the ROI of digital advertising?

Although Helene has the idea that StaidCorp must go digital, she's unable to answer a single question posed by the exploration team. By allowing the exploration team the time to answer their questions, Helene expects them to deliver a well-defined digital path to bring StaidCorp back into the black.

Helene is starting to see the value of taking time for applied research before engaging the larger team with a vague mandate.

Key Takeaways

1. The *Agile Manifesto* philosophy doesn't address some real-world difficulties in Agile development cycles.
2. The most common Agile challenge is beginning a sprint when the targeted stories are inadequately understood. When this occurs, the team stops sprinting and must dig for answers.
3. The Agile work cycle appears to be a continuous productivity loop. The need for deep thinking about especially complicated feature sets is implicit in the Agile workflow.
4. Agile is not a shortcut to producing better software in a shorter time. Successful Agile sprints require at least an equal amount of discovery.
5. Sprints fail during the planning process when Product teams and developers overlook the complexity of seemingly simple stories.
6. The benefit of a Waterfall approach is that the exhaustive upfront study ensures every piece of the system is considered.
7. The downfall of Waterfall is the lack of engineers on the team who may identify infeasible solutions.
8. Talented multidisciplinary exploration teams perform just enough applied research to understand the contours of a potential project.
9. Engaging a small exploration team is a small commitment that may lead to a no-go decision if the ROI is insufficient.
10. Exploration teams must include senior-level employees typically in high demand for other profit-generating projects. Therefore, budgeting must include funding for a permanent discovery team.

CHAPTER 5

A Closer Look

Obstacles to Agile

Agile is merely a sensible way to chip away at large chunks of work, not a panacea to cure all corporate ills. Organizational dysfunction manifests in myriad ways, many of which result in failed Agile sprints. The first step in achieving agility is to recognize and address the issues in a company that prevent heads-down work.

Humans aren't designed to do two things at once except for walking and chewing gum. Rather, people are unable to simultaneously *concentrate* on two things. No matter how much a teenager claims superhuman multitasking abilities, they are merely devoting small slices of time to multiple endeavors, likely performing well on none of them.

Almost every state in America, and many other countries, has distracted driving laws prohibiting people from texting while driving (Schwartz, "Is Texting and Driving Illegal?"). Teenagers bent on texting while driving need to travel to Montana, virtually the only state lacking distracted driving laws.

The nearly global enforcement of distracted driving rules acknowledges the deadliness of multitasking while operating a vehicle. Most other distractions aren't outlawed because their outcomes are more benign. Still, distractions generally lead to subpar results, regardless of the potential loss of life.

Workers, especially those who sit in an office, face distractions all the time. Although it's something of an exaggeration, many people claim that the office is no place to perform actual work. Between e-mail, phone calls, messaging apps, noisy coworkers, and meeting happy managers, it's a wonder that office workers produce anything whatsoever.

Agile sprints are intended to address the problem of distracted workers. When an Agile team is sprinting, they are supposed to work heads-down without disturbance. If a company heeds the rules of Agile, it's generally understood that sprinting employees are not available for anything else until the sprint ends.

Chapter 4 addresses sprint failures caused by insufficient upfront discovery. The people on the sprint team must stop and dig for answers when user stories aren't fully considered before a sprint starts. This need to stop and dig for answers is a distraction, not to mention a time sink.

Other common types of distraction, detailed in this chapter, are even more pernicious than the lack of upfront discovery.

Management Disrespecting Sanctity of Iterations

One of the important rules of iterative work is the immutability of the plan. That is, once the stakeholders agree upon the user stories for the sprint, the stories do not change after the sprint begins.

Managers may not sneak in additional stories. The formal term for this type of gilding the lily is *scope creep*, meaning that management increases the team's obligations by piling on unsanctioned stories. Scope creep is typically caused by human forgetfulness rather than nefariousness. Managers or customers may overlook an important piece of work and cajole the team to slip the additional work into the sprint. Scope creep is a slippery slope. Once a team gives in to demands, it becomes harder to refuse similar requests in the future.

What enables a sprint team to refuse additional work? After all, business needs change all the time. What may have been important yesterday may be usurped by something else today. Surely, a sprint should reflect the most important work at the moment.

The saving grace of the immutable sprint is the short cycle for the work. It's much simpler to refuse changes to a sprint when its duration is only a week or two. When the sprint ends, it's legitimate for changed business priorities to trigger an entirely unexpected new set of user stories.

Why Interrupting Sprints Is Inadvisable

If the business landscape changes more rapidly than a sprint cycle, isn't it better to have the work reflect the new problems? Is this *immutability of an active sprint* insistence merely the edict of beleaguered developers and not a real necessity?

No, and no, for three very good reasons:

1. **Inability to measure success**—Self-managing teams value the reflective postmortem after each sprint when the team discusses how to perform better the next time. If the rug is pulled out by swapping work mid-sprint, the team loses the ability to keep score. Keeping score is about more than computing sprint velocity by adding up story points. The intrinsic joy a team feels by meeting its obligations gets lost when the team loses its autonomy.

2. **Cognitive overload**—When a wrench is tossed into the sprint, professional teams stop, consider the new problems, and make the best of it. Although the team cannot make the proverbial lemonade from lemons, they do their best to accommodate their new situation. The team loses their heads-down focus because the sprint changes require the sprinting to temporarily stop to understand and absorb the new work.

3. **Morale problems**—Saving the worst for last, changes to a sprint are demoralizing. Most professionals value controlling their work as the key to job satisfaction. Uncertainty about the day's work unsettles all but the most schizophrenic workers. When management or a customer runs roughshod over a self-managing team, they no longer call their own shots, and therefore, lose one of their keys to job contentment.

A Failed Sprint Scenario

A startup is reinventing itself. After some contentious marketing-led sessions, the Management team has agreed upon a new mission statement, a new value proposition, and an overall strategy. With an opinionated

Management team, reaching a consensus about such fundamental issues is a heavy lift. Therefore, Marketing structured it as a two-week sprint. Although each participant lost some sleep and suffered bumps and bruises, the team met their goals. Mission accomplished.

With this hard work out of the way, the Marketing team is now sprinting to insert the new messaging into the corporate slide decks and website. The company is introducing a new product in a month. Marketing wants their messaging and design ready for the new product rollout. As they envision the work, they will devote this two-week sprint to ensuring consistency of messaging in their print and digital materials.

Marketing will use their third two-week sprint to work alongside a designer to ensure the graphics are consistent across their materials.

A new head of Sales joined the company shortly after the Management team had produced their mission statement, value proposition, and strategy. When she was interviewing for the position, the CEO loved her, but she did nothing to endear herself to the other executives with whom she spoke. She said she intended to ruffle feathers, question the other managers' productivity, and do whatever it takes to hit ambitious sales goals. The CEO was thrilled to finally have a sales leader with a cutthroat attitude after years of team players who routinely missed their sales targets.

True to her word, the new head of Sales reviewed the mission statement, value proposition, and strategy, declaring all of them inadequate. She complained to the CEO that the constraints of the team's thinking compromise her ability to meet her quarterly sales goals.

Loathe to alienate his new hotshot head of Sales, the CEO instructs the Marketing team to incorporate the Sales head's revisions into their sprint. Marketing quickly realizes that the revisions are a complete rewrite that directly opposes much of what the Management team already decided. Although a few of the new head of Sales' points have merit, the Marketing team disagrees with most of them. They think the revisions reek of a new employee who lacks an understanding of the company and its products.

The time that would have been spent completing their sprint goals is devoted to new rounds of Management team squabbling. Ultimately, the Management team comes to an agreement, and the final mission statement, value proposition, and strategy are similar to the original incarnation.

Unfortunately, Marketing declares their sprint a failure because they accomplished none of their goals of aligning their slides and website with the new messaging. All the time they would have spent finishing the work of the sprint was devoted to an unnecessary revisiting of completed work.

Marketing will not have enough time to complete the design work before the product rollout. Although the team had an inflexible schedule, they felt confident and excited about their plan. The last-minute changes usurp the team's self-management and prevent them from maximizing the marketing around the new product rollout. The Marketing team is demoralized.

The Trickiness of Interdependent Sprints

In most cases, the failure of a two-week sprint isn't especially damaging because there's only so much that's lost in a short iteration. On the other hand, allowing work that's destined to fail to continue for months or years can sink a company. In the case of the second Marketing sprint, the inability to incorporate the new mission statement and value proposition into the marketing slides and website results in cascading failure. The subsequent sprint that is intended to unify the design across the marketing materials will not begin before the product is released. Consequently, insufficient marketing may cause the new product to miss its sales projections.

Although Marketing faced an unnecessary obstacle, they didn't coordinate well enough with the Product team. Marketing's just-in-time approach to finishing their collateral to coincide with the new product release leaves no room for failure or unexpected wrenches in the works. The failure of Marketing's second sprint makes it impossible for their third sprint to succeed. Building slack into the schedule for important interdependent sprints allows for the recovery from an unexpected failure without scuttling the entire mission.

Implications of Too Much Interruption

Aside from a preponderance of introversion, software developers tend to favor working from home because it enables them to have uninterrupted blocks of concentration. The most obvious implication of interruptions is that work isn't completed.

As noted at the beginning of this chapter, humans aren't built to multitask. Humans are built to focus. Internet-fueled doom-scrolling trains people not to focus. The distractedness of today's adults gave rise to the self-help publishing category about focusing with books about finding one's flow state, gaming one's productivity, and emulating legendary high producers like Bill Gates and Elon Musk.

A more subtle implication of excessive interruption is the damage caused by allowing reactionary responses to overpower corporate strategy. Ideally, an underlying business strategy guides workers, even though they may be forced to stray because of more immediate concerns. More simply, short-term pressures often conflict with long-term goals. Anyone who's worked at a struggling company probably has a laundry list of examples like these where short-term pragmatism trumped long-term strategy:

1. An important potential customer makes a missing feature a condition of a sale. Even though the strategically inadvisable feature was previously deep-sixed, the feckless CEO strongarms the Engineering team to squeeze it into a release.
2. A VP of Sales is preparing to visit an important customer who just complained bitterly about a usability issue. Although the Product team acknowledges the usability issue, it has a low priority because the Engineering team has more important issues to address first. The VP of Sales pushes for a quick modification to mollify the customer because it will demonstrate commitment and likely result in add-on business.
3. A CEO has some free time over a weekend and fires up her company's product. She finds something she considers a bug. Based on actual customer usage, the Product team is aware of the issue and explains it's a low-priority usability issue. The CEO pulls rank and demands it be addressed with an emergency patch.

A sprint cycle is usually so short that most interruptions are borne from emergencies. High-severity bugs and usability issues may derail even the most disciplined product teams.

Fires and Firefighting

Startups are motivated by youthful energy, fueled by adrenaline, and supplemented by caffeine. The frenetic pace of a startup cannot be sustained forever. If a company remains a startup too long, it will either burn through its cash or the original team will become too long in the tooth to muster the same enthusiasm that powered its early victories. Or both. Companies that successfully navigate the transition from a startup to a growth phase are forced to reconsider their approach to *all hands on deck* events.

The preeminent all-consuming events for startups are potentially catastrophic, customer-affecting events, aka *fires*. For example, when a startup's biggest, and possibly sole, customer phones the CEO in a rage to report their data have suddenly gone absent without official leave (AWOL), there's no question that it's a four-alarm fire.

In almost all fires associated with a company's technology, the most valuable firefighters are often working heads-down in a sprint. If a customer is unable to use the company's product because of this issue and cannot conduct their business, a responsible team must abandon their sprint and go into firefighting mode. The unfortunate outcome of fires is the disruption of planned work and the slippage of delivery schedules. Every company that delivers software on an aggressive schedule has the occasional fire. When fires become routine events, it indicates deeper problems.

Customer-affecting events aren't the only types of corporate fires requiring a massive response. From the sales side, the loss of an important customer or the disintegration of a sure-thing deal is a revenue-affecting event with immense potential implications. Companies budget based on a sales forecast. When a structural leg of the sales forecast collapses, the company risks missing revenue targets. The firefighting of a sales loss is often a mad scramble to make up for the scuttled deal with additional sales to avoid having to reset year-end expectations and avoid layoffs.

In real life, about 65 percent of the nation's fire departments are entirely or mostly composed of volunteers (Fahy et al. 2022). These brave volunteers put their own lives aside when called to fight fires. Similarly, firefighters at startups have regular jobs that get tossed aside when it's time to douse the flames.

In real life, fires are mesmerizing events that attract neighbors who want to help. Similarly, those not directly responsible for extinguishing the fire often act in supporting roles until the crisis passes. Startups typically employ an *it takes a village* approach to attack crises and engage most if not all of their employees. This all-consuming firefighting may succeed, but it comes at a great cost. Not only is the entire company diverted from their regular responsibilities, but employees may start to crave the adrenaline of fighting a huge blaze.

Developing fire containment plans and procedures designed to quickly identify the key players helps to contain fires to only essential personnel. By not engaging bystanders in fires, even small companies may continue forward progress while also fighting fires.

No company can afford to expend all its resources on a single fire. Although a fire remains an important and potentially catastrophic event, most companies have multiple customers and deadlines that can't be derailed. A company cannot afford to marshal the entire team to fight fires. However, it's exceedingly difficult to change all-consuming firefighting behavior for the following reasons, which also happen to represent the ingredients of fire:

1. **Oxygen**—Actual fires require oxygen in the atmosphere. The atmosphere at a startup is all about heroics, and nothing illustrates it better than individuals saving the day. It's been well documented that a minority of firefighters become arsonists, possibly for the thrill of the blaze and the recognition of extinguishing it. Although company employees aren't intentionally wreaking havoc on their customers, the underlying culture may not encourage employees to avoid fires.

2. **Fuel**—One of the essential components of a fire is the presence of material that will burn. The corporate equivalent of fuel are weaknesses that are vulnerable to dysfunction. In the sales context, prespending against a deal before the contract is signed is fuel for a fire. Similarly, the loss of a customer almost always has a forewarning which, if not heeded, is fuel for a budgetary fire.

The technical equivalent of fuel is weakness in the codebase. Every team faces pragmatic challenges to release software before it's perfect. Experienced engineering leaders learn the appropriate corners to cut to deliver software on time. These same engineering leaders are also responsible enough to keep track of these cut corners, aka *technical debt*, to properly address them when time permits. The accrued technical debt that isn't paid down is like a gasoline can; neither the technical debt nor the gasoline will spontaneously combust, but their absence will prevent fires.

3. **Heat**—Although oxygen and fuel are two essential ingredients of fire, there will be no fire without a source of heat. The most likely source of heat in a company fire is human error. The pressure to release software in complicated hosting configurations often results in production surprises that didn't occur in preproduction environments.

Here's how a company contains its fires. The following practices eliminate or reduce the elements that compose a fire.

1. **Culture**—Unlearning a culture of heroism is hard. However, the fire is containable, and the company won't be derailed if managers assemble small, multidisciplinary teams. A firefighting team requires the technical skills to address the issue, the business savvy to craft a schedule for the fix, and effective communication skills to keep stakeholders informed.

2. **Prioritization**—Engineers know the risks of un-repaid technical debt. In the push for new features, the paydown of debt that yields no visible customer benefit often becomes a low priority to those outside the Engineering team. In the quest for the latest whiz-bang feature that blows away the competition, Product Management often develops an *out-of-sight, out-of-mind* mentality about technical debt and deprioritizes it. Instead of playing Chicken Little about the potential dangers of technical debt, Engineering does better by highlighting the benefits of addressing technical debt with metrics. For example, 20 percent better throughput or 25 percent less code complexity. Explaining the positive impact of addressing technical

debt ensures it will be prioritized fairly. The removal of technical debt is akin to starving a fire of its fuel.

3. **Process and quality**—As companies grow and releases become more complicated, automation becomes an essential tool to reduce human error. Automatically executing an ever-expanding library of tests when code is merged provides immediate feedback. If any of the tests fail, Engineering makes fixes until the tests pass. In addition, although most startups test their software, few have employees who focus solely on quality; this becomes a key role in a growth company. Quality assurance is concerned with validating that proposed engineering solutions address customer problems without introducing unnecessary product complexity—and the potential for additional bugs.

It is unrealistic to expect that any one plan will eliminate fires. Therefore, building some slack into schedules seems reasonable to account for unexpected events. Unfortunately, planning for fires is impossible because they are inherently chaotic events that defy the best-laid plans. Still, a game plan outlining the participants and responsibilities provides some safe harbor when the house is burning. Ideally, companies avoid derailment by following a prescribed set of firefighting steps.

Compartmentalizing a Fire

It is too late to figure out how to respond when a fire is blazing. Having a playbook that dictates the firefighting process gives companies a logical set of steps when the stress of a fire might otherwise force reactive solutions. A well-considered process might enable small companies to survive fires without losing too much ground. Playbooks help teams to maintain focus when fires threaten to upend everything. For example, designing a process where the reproduction of the issue, triage, and outward communication occurs outside of Engineering spreads the burden of firefighting across the company. Ultimately, it may take Engineering time to fix a problem, but the delay in its involvement allows forward development progress for as long as possible.

Postmortem Examinations

When a real fire has been reduced to smoking embers, there's an investigation to determine its cause. The investigation results hopefully provide sufficient education to avoid similar fires in the future and determine the insurance payout. It behooves a company to perform the same sort of *postmortem* investigation for mostly the same reasons.

Often, a company's firefighters have lost so much ground that they want to forget about the fire and return to their regularly scheduled responsibilities. Furthermore, producing postmortem fire reports usually requires an admission of culpability, which makes many people uncomfortable. To avoid similar future fires, managers must demand the accountability of a postmortem report. Managers who carefully read and question the content of these reports may gain important insights.

Reading Between the Postmortem Lines

Nontechnical postmortem explanations of technical failures have become the expected denouement of catastrophic events. When the servers relying on U.S. East AWS hosting all go down, AWS issues an explanation. When 70 million customer records are breached, Target issued its own postmortem explanation.

Interestingly, the actual details of immense failures are frequently mundane, embarrassing human errors like forgetting a semicolon in a script file or overlooking easily avoidable code vulnerabilities. An appropriately self-flagellating e-mail is often sufficient for forgiveness. After all, humans are fallible, and a willingness to identify the root cause feels to many like taking ownership.

Smart managers demand more than an exposition of a problem's origins. They want plans for the prevention of the same problems in the future. Crowing about grandiose plans to right all the wrongs of the catastrophe is one thing, but implementing the plan requires much more time and energy than the glib rhapsodizing in a postmortem report.

The follow-through on a postmortem report is the hidden time-sink of fires. The catastrophe itself is already a significant distraction and the cause of missed sprint goals. Preventing future fires of the same type often requires an even more painful investment of resources.

Repeatedly Fighting the Same Fire

Human mistakes will occur until artificial intelligence bots take over human jobs. That's just the nature of humans running the show. Although humans are destined to make mistakes, humans are not destined to repeat the same mistakes. Generally, companies are forgiven a human-fueled gaffe if a sufficiently groveling postmortem report accompanies it. Patience wears thin, however, when a company repeats the same mistakes because it hasn't taken the steps to fix the problems.

Typically, postmortem reports of episodes repeating the same mistake will mask the circumstances to avoid the embarrassing admission of not having fixed the problem the first time. Bloodhound-nosed managers will demand an in-depth explanation of the root causes if they smell the rottenness of a repeated mistake. These insistent managers may not like what they hear.

In the best case, the same issue causes recurrent fires because time wasn't devoted to repairing simple problems. In the worst case, fixing fire-related problems is more expensive than fires.

A couple of examples help to illustrate the fire/fix cost calculus:

1. A longstanding, financially important customer leaves for a competitor. This departure leaves an immense hole in the budget that sales scrambles to fill. The postmortem report reveals the software doesn't accommodate the expanded needs of the customer's business. The customer clearly communicated their dissatisfaction for the past year.

   Customers constantly push vendors to expand the footprint of products to support increasingly broad new business requirements. For example, an accounting software company may receive a request from a customer to automatically build an executive slide deck to present financial numbers to investors. Although the accounting software company acknowledges the value of the request, they prefer spending their time improving the product's accounting features. Understandably, a vendor like the accounting software company wants to focus on the narrow product in their sweet spot—the accounting software, instead of building a fancy reporting system. Equally understandably, customers value all-in-one solutions that seamlessly address all their needs.

In this case, Sales didn't recognize the seriousness of the customer's threat. Sales believed that the customer was so firmly entrenched that leaving for another vendor would be more painful than dealing with the lack of new functionality. A fatal miscalculation.

When customers demand product expansion that isn't part of the vendor's strategic direction, the best approach is to integrate with another company's product that provides the needed functionality. In the accounting software company example, the appropriate solution is integrating with a third party to build attractive slide presentations. The worst approach is for the company to bury its head in the sand, pretending it never heard the request.

The customer specified what they needed. Not only didn't the company address the customer's needs, but they also didn't anticipate losing the customer. After losing the customer, the company may lose the impetus to build the integration, leaving the door open for additional customer exodus.

Integrations are, at best, difficult, and at worst, excruciating. However, the cost of integrating is generally significantly lower than building something new from scratch. In terms of cost calculus, the best decision is to build integrations instead of risking losing lucrative customers.

2. Reading multiple postmortem reports, an astute CEO deduces that an important product feature is causing a disproportionate number of fires. Due to time constraints, Engineering took too many shortcuts over the years in this heavily trafficked area of the code. Furthermore, the team was never allowed the time to properly refactor the code and fix the problems. Consequently, Engineering has built a sprawling city on top of a swampy foundation.

The code is now so complex that even seemingly benign enhancements tend to break the software in unexpected places. Junior developers are reluctant to touch this Bermuda Triangle area of the product when even senior developers get tangled in the byzantine code.

The most fraught words a CEO hears from Engineering are, "We need a complete software re-architecture." Visions of months, possibly years, of software rewriting resulting in a lesser-featured, buggy release dance like rotten sugarplums before the CEO's eyes. In this case, however, it sure sounds like this part of the product needs a complete redo.

The Cost of Rearchitecture

Many homeowners have experienced snowballing renovation projects. Replacing the wood on a front porch may reveal rotten subflooring, which may uncover a cracked foundation. Suddenly, the simple wood replacement turns into a whole-house teardown.

Technical projects built on flimsy foundations have a way of multiplying in the same way. Pieces of the software tied to one another without well-defined interfaces may result in interrelationships that are impossible to separate. Therefore, redoing one part of the software may mushroom into redoing the whole kit and caboodle.

Regardless of the precise application, from housing to software, rearchitecture projects often contain these pitfalls:

1. **Time/cost overruns**—Very large projects are difficult to accurately estimate. If a redo project is approached with an Agile mindset, the time and cost will be reevaluated and refined after each milestone. In most cases, redo projects cost more and take more time than was initially estimated.
2. **Minimal first versions**—A family squeezed into a small Airbnb while their house is being rebuilt are likely to move back in before the landscaping is completed and the light fixtures are installed. Eventually, the builder will finish the final touches, but it may take some time.

   From a software perspective, any new product's first version is invariably less featured than the legacy product it replaces. Customers accustomed to the full-featured product may grouse until parity is achieved in the new product.

3. **Bugginess**—Auto experts advise against purchasing the first model year of a new car. Getting the kinks out of a new car sometimes takes until the second or third model year. Similarly, a large software release will invariably be buggy.

4. **Lost opportunity cost**—Instead of building new features into a product, a company deciding to rebuild from scratch makes a strategic long-term decision. Forgoing new features on a flimsy foundation in favor of fewer features on a firm foundation is often a bitter pill for customers to swallow.

The steep costs of a product redo may be justified by the higher costs of not doing anything and losing customers. Seldom are these decisions a slam dunk. Rearchitecture projects require clear-eyed justification because they have so many potential downsides.

Process Issues Hamper Agility

This chapter presents two different kinds of fires. The first fire has technical origins for Engineering to address. The second fire is a scramble for Sales to recover from the loss of a *sure-thing* deal. Better processes may have prevented or minimized both of these fires.

Customer Churn

The first situation, where a customer expressed their dissatisfaction and ultimately left, could have been avoided by proactively addressing the complaints. Most Customer Success teams are skilled at recognizing potential customer churn and taking measures to prevent it. If, however, the customer's complaints never reached Customer Success, it's possible that the risk was never fully understood.

The sales cycle is sometimes so long with enterprise software that the salesperson develops a personal relationship with the customer along the way. Consequently, after the sale closes, the customer may continue to bring their issues directly to the salesperson. The customer likely expects the salesperson to act as the funnel, routing issues to the appropriate internal team.

The salesperson may not have recognized the customer churn risk in part because that's not the job of sales. When the customer asked why the software couldn't accommodate a new need, the salesperson may have recommended the customer buy a solution from another vendor rather than pass the issue along to Customer Success.

A better process might have preserved this customer. Instead, losing the customer upended progress while the Sales team tried to make up the budget shortfall.

Culture of Testing

Technical fires are the most common type of software company catastrophe. The elimination of bugs also starves fires of fuel. Bugs are killed through comprehensive testing. Surprisingly, many Engineering teams don't include unit tests that fully exercise new code in their development process.

Even if a Software team doesn't use TDD and writes tests before writing code, tests are still mandatory. Writing unit tests that verify code in isolation identifies problems from the outset and uncovers new bugs when the code is changed. Although test development is more of a culture than a process, once an engineering team agrees to require tests, their inclusion becomes a part of the normal development process.

Boy Scouts have a rule that demands they leave a campsite cleaner than they found it. With Boy Scouting, it's all about citizenship and responsibility. The Boy Scout rule of programming means that developers should leave the code in better condition than they found it. For old code without tests, applying the Boy Scout rule suggests including tests to improve the codebase.

The Agility Quiz

Agility is a hard-won characteristic of functional organizations. Unfortunately, as this chapter illustrates, agility is also a mixed blessing. All manner of calamities, bad luck, willful sabotage, and damaged processes conspire to rob companies of their agility.

The following quiz requires no late-night cramming. Simply count your yeses and noes and refer to the scale at the end.

1. Does upper management respect work in progress and refrain from making urgent requests?
2. When a team is working heads-down, are they empowered to refuse new work until they reach a stopping point?
3. Is the work of teams guided more by strategic direction than short-term tactical concerns?
4. Has your company been working at a relaxed pace to bring carefully designed, well-tested products to market?
5. Are teams provided the space and time to refactor shortcuts taken in earlier iterations?
6. Are processes in place to effectively recognize and promptly address customer complaints?
7. Are emergency processes in place that attempt to contain the response to a small group of employees?
8. Does your company emphasize group collaboration and success over individual heroics?
9. Does your company commit to a budget but revisit it regularly to align spending with actual sales?
10. Does your company require postmortem reports after a fire?
11. Are the postmortem reports scrutinized and questioned by management?
12. Are employees given the time to address the fire prevention measures they identify in the aftermath of calamitous events?
13. Are employees willing to take the time to fully address any fire prevention recommendations they make?
14. Are fires in your company seldom repeats of the same problem?
15. Are the products your company ships fully covered with tests?

Scoring the Agility Quiz

0–5 yeses: Time for a reckoning. A score this low suggests a company is constantly inundated with unexpected problems that cause missed deliverables and customer dissatisfaction. Furthermore, employee morale may be so low that attrition compounds the problems.

6–10 yeses: Plenty of room for improvement, but a company with this score is on the right path. There may be too many fires that aren't well-contained. By addressing root cause issues and giving teams the space to self-manage, this company may achieve real agility.

11–15 yeses: Congratulations. Unexpected catastrophes seldom derail this company. When they do occur, fires are well contained. Teams are provided the time and support to address the recommendations of postmortem fire reports. Teams are also provided the time to correct shortcuts and refactor work from previous sprints.

Key Takeaways

1. Humans are not efficient multitaskers. Distracted driving laws recognize the danger of multitasking while operating a vehicle.
2. Managers driven by tactical emergencies may push teams to change course mid-sprint. The short duration of sprints provides teams the ammunition to refuse any changes once the sprint begins.
3. The interruption of a sprint is damaging because it makes the sprint immeasurable. Additionally, interrupted sprints cause cognitive overload.
4. Failed sprints affect team morale.
5. Fires are often all-consuming events at small companies. However, no company can afford to involve too many people in firefighting because it derails forward progress.
6. The most well-known fires involve technical breaches or server failures, but nontechnical fires can be just as calamitous.
7. Astute managers demand postmortem reports that describe the causes of fires and pay close attention to them to determine if the fires represent a recurrence of problems that were never properly addressed.
8. Although fires may derail progress, following through on addressing root cause problems helps ensure the same problems aren't repeated. Unfortunately, root cause mitigation may be more expensive than the fires.

9. In general, rearchitecting any aspect of a product may be extraordinarily expensive. However, more fires will probably occur by patching a deficient product instead of fixing it.

10. Adopting processes that foster interteam communications helps to identify and address problems before they become urgent.

CHAPTER 6

Measuring Success

Although Agile provides teams a way to measure the success of their sprints, these internal tools, like story points, aren't intended for management's eyes. Instead, objectives and metrics provide a better way for those who don't belong to a team to recognize progress or lack thereof.

Story Points in Detail

As a brief refresher, story points are the numbers assigned to stories to assess their relative size. Although a story size may obliquely translate to its implementation time, story points are intentionally abstract. Story point estimation aims to correctly size stories relative to one another. Complex stories may receive more points than simple stories. Two stories with the same implementation complexity should be assigned the same points.

Teams may devise any story point scale they wish. One common story point scale is T-shirt sizing—XS, S, M, L, XL, and XXL. Another of the most common story point systems is prime numbers up to 11—1, 2, 3, 5, 7, and 11. Stories awarded one point may be trivial and quick, while those receiving an 11 are hairy and difficult. If estimations are correct, 11 one-point stories should take the same time to complete as one 11-point story. Consistently assigning story points over time is, perhaps, the biggest challenge of this type of estimation. Consistency of story point estimation is also an absolute requirement or the whole thing falls apart.

Engineering teams use story point estimation to understand their capacity. A team may discover over several sprints that they usually finish 24 story points per sprint. Another larger team may complete 40 story points. A team using a different scale may complete 100 story points. The number of points is much less important than a team's ability to consistently complete roughly the same number of points in each sprint. The team's *velocity* is the number of points completed in a sprint.

Story point velocity is a brittle metric. Any changes in team composition, like adding, subtracting, or swapping teammates, will affect velocity. Furthermore, inconsistency in story point assignment over several sprints makes it impossible to compute velocity.

Story points and velocity are effective ways for Product Management and Engineering to communicate. When an Engineering team estimates their stories, they can tell the Product Manager how many points they can complete. Product Management is then free to choose stories whose points add up to the total.

One of the most common questions about story points is their relationship to calendar time. If a five-person team can complete 50 story points in a two-week sprint, it's easy to do the math and compute that the average story points per developer are 10, and each story point reflects eight hours of work. This computation of story points to actual time is a slippery slope.

Do Not Fall Into the Story Point Trap

Quantifying story points into actual hours is dangerous. If management gets ahold of story point estimates and does the math, all manner of crazy shenanigans may result. For example, if a CEO is unhappy with the rate of new feature releases, she might say, "If we increase the team size by 50 percent, this will give us an extra 20 story points, which means we will have space for these extra features." Another CEO might dole out end-of-year bonuses based on each employee's percentage of the total story points achieved in the year.

There are plenty of reasons why these CEOs are wrong. For one, any change to team composition changes the team's capacity. It is incorrect that adding people to a team linearly increases its capacity. Introducing new employees initially *decreases* overall team productivity because training and mentoring replace some heads-down work.

Expanding a team may permanently decrease its capacity because of the communication overhead. In the early days of Amazon, Jeff Bezos instituted the two-pizza rule: Every internal team must be small enough so no more than two pizzas are required to feed them (Hern 2018). The two-pizza rule acknowledges the communication challenges of large teams. When an Amazon team reaches the two-pizza limit, they create a new team instead of expanding the current team. Amazon's two-pizza rule persists to this day.

Story Points Are for Internal Team Use

Workers are generally allergic to providing date estimates for their work. Estimates become firm commitments when dates are communicated to customers, even if there's no business necessity to deliver on that date. Invariably, promising delivery of specific features on a specific date will require compromises.

If the delivery date is unbendable and the estimate is incorrect, the Engineering team may be forced to cut corners. Alternatively, the Engineering team works until the delivery date, and the Testing team doesn't have sufficient time to guarantee a robust product. If the date is fungible and it's pushed back, the Engineering team will be accused of not hitting its deliverables. Committing to a wide date range instead of a specific date is a better delivery strategy. The best delivery strategy is to avoid date commitments for functionality that isn't business-critical. There is no upside to providing date estimates for employees who produce customer-consumable content.

The abstract nature of story points allows some wiggle room on hard dates. Story points estimate a team's capacity to finish stories within a specified time. Story point estimation seems a reasonable compromise between the date-wary content producers and the beleaguered customer-facing employees hounded by customers for firm dates.

As much as employees prefer the laissez-faire, "It will be ready when it's ready," approach to estimation, this doesn't fly with the customer-facing sides of businesses. For one, coordination between the Marketing, Sales, Support, and Product teams requires at least some internal estimates.

However, a CEO's mere mention of story points is reason enough for employees to reject story point estimation. There are well-documented cases of senior executives weaponizing internal metrics to assess individual employee productivity.

An example of gross misuse of internal metrics occurred with Elon Musk's takeover of Twitter (now X) when he used GitHub commits and accompanying comments to rank employees based on their productivity (Lavallee 2022).

To better understand Musk's intentions, nonprogrammers require a few definitions. Programmers store the code they write in source code repositories that exist in a central location. *GitHub* is a popular cloud-based source code repository. A programmer may write code on their local computer but wants to ensure it also exists elsewhere, much like using Dropbox to keep files safe from a hard drive crash. When the programmer finishes writing a chunk of code, they *commit* it to GitHub. Many teams insist on having other programmers review the work to ensure its quality before the commit is permitted. Also, responsible programmers write descriptive comments describing the purpose of the new code.

Although Musk is plenty intelligent, he's not a software developer. His attempt to judge programmer productivity based on code commits to a version control system is counterproductive. Programmers are smart, too. If they're being evaluated on code commits, they will make more commits and embellish them with impressive, hifalutin comments.

When executives abuse internal metrics, employees will find ways to game the numbers. For example, if a CEO wants to base compensation on the completion of story points, employees will fudge the numbers. Workers can complete more story points by assigning higher point values to trivial issues. Employees will avoid truly complex issues with high story points.

When micromanagers get their fingers into story points, rest assured that this type of estimation loses all its utility.

Middle Management Needs to Administer Down and Report Up

When someone in the C-suite starts sniffing around at the team members' individual productivity, it's often because the Department Manager isn't providing enough transparency regarding schedules, goals, and achievements. A manager ineffectively reporting up to her managers without sufficient data leads them to demand numbers to quantify productivity or lack thereof.

Most managers have an acute understanding of the leaders and slackers on their teams. These managers know that it takes all types to make a team. Having a balance of fast, reckless whirling dervishes mixed with ruminative, meticulous sticklers often yields robust products delivered in a reasonable time frame. Hands-on managers know the strengths and weaknesses of each employee even without tallying numeric metrics.

Savvy managers routinely gain enough understanding of new projects to match the work to the workers' strengths. For example, when a patient with a unique medical condition calls for an appointment, the scheduler tries to find the doctor with the most relevant experience. If there are multiple qualified doctors, the urgency of the appointment will influence the scheduler to choose the one with the earliest availability.

The scheduler in a medical practice is a middle manager who handles customer appointments and answers to doctors. If a patient with an enlarged prostate insists on receiving same-day service, the scheduler may not find the perfect fit because of the need for expedience.

Even in creative fields, managers use the same qualification and time window logic to match the work with the worker. Take a profession as inherently immeasurable as art. Art benefactors are middle managers who know the go-to person for time-sensitive work.

In his bestselling biography, *Leonardo da Vinci*, Walter Isaacson immerses himself in 15th-century Italy. Studying da Vinci's sketchbooks and works of art, Isaacson paints a picture of a brilliant and distractable artist. Occasionally, da Vinci was passed over for big jobs by his benefactor, Lorenzo de' Medici. For example, the Sistine Chapel ceiling commission went to Michelangelo, one of da Vinci's contemporaries (Isaacson 2017, 356).

It's easy to imagine Lorenzo de' Medici's assessment of Leonardo da Vinci:

Leo has great attention to detail. His drawings of the human anatomy are astonishingly realistic. That is, if Leo completes his work. I've seldom experienced a more distractable employee. Leo will start drawing an arm, get excited about the way water flows in the river, and abandon his original drawing. While his innate talent is indisputable, his disciple is lacking. He has a pattern of leaving half-finished works lying around as if he expects others to complete them.

Leo is also a perfectionist which, I think, is a big part of his problem. When the going gets tough and Leo can't get it absolutely correct, he'll put his painting on the shelf. He's been working on this painting he calls "Mona Lisa" for almost a decade. I keep telling him to finish it, already. He's letting great get in the way of good.

His pal Michelangelo, on the other hand, is an absolute workhorse. He chiseled out "David" in the time Leo was dithering with his sketchbook. When I need work done tout de suite, I look to Michelangelo. Leo was miffed when I gave Michelangelo the Sistine Chapel ceiling. Although it took Michelangelo four years to complete the ceiling, I knew Leo would never have finished it.

If de' Medici had upcoming work requiring precise, scientific anatomical drawings, he'd most certainly want to use da Vinci provided the deadline wasn't too tight. Otherwise, he'd go with Michelangelo, who was no slouch in the realistic representation of the human form. If a church was seeking a graceful religious painting, de' Medici might go with the talented but less renowned Sandro Botticelli. de' Medici understands each artist well enough to play to their strengths so they can deliver spectacular results. There's no need for de' Medici to provide the reasoning for his scheduling to his customers.

Like de' Medici, managers wary of upper management meddling may hide the inner workings of their teams and let the results speak for themselves. This strategy of presenting the sausage but hiding the sausage-making may be acceptable only if the results are stupendous. Senior managers may try to backseat drive the process if they're offered too much behind-the-scenes information. The middle manager must provide the right balance of transparency and opacity.

When a middle manager reports the results of a project to their boss and hides the progressive details, the boss lacks the context to understand the magnitude of the accomplishment. For example, if de' Medici kept the Sistine Chapel priests in the dark about the ceiling project's ongoing progress only to report that Michelangelo finished it after four years, the priests would probably have questions. Instead of celebrating Michelangelo's magnificent accomplishment, the priest would probably grouse, "Sure, it's beautiful but I was expecting the ceiling to be finished two years ago. de' Medici should have put da Vinci on the project as a second painter so that they could finish on time."

Unless specific measures are in place that define success and failure, senior management will question why the team didn't deliver more.

Why Management Wants Metrics

It's fair game to bash managers who inappropriately use internal metrics to unfairly evaluate employees. However, senior managers will grasp at whatever's available when they have no visibility into the reasons why a team is underperforming.

Scenario: Metric-Driven Teams Versus Status Report-Driven Teams

A company steals a successful salesperson from a direct competitor. Ordinarily, sales jobs are a revolving door where success or failure hinges on a few well-defined metrics. The salesperson flounders in her new position, missing all her sales targets. In this case, however, the CEO knows this employee is a top-notch sales professional. The CEO also realizes that Sales is the company's only metric-driven department.

The Marketing, Product, Engineering, Support, Human Resources, and Finance teams provide looser reporting that makes it difficult to gauge the teams' performance. Consequently, the conundrum of the underperforming salesperson remains a mystery. The CEO is unable to determine if failures in other parts of the company are preventing the salesperson from reaching her targets or if there's some hidden problem in the Sales organization.

The VP of Sales comes to senior management meetings with spreadsheets that drill into individual salespeople's performance against the projected plan. The other departments provide status reports of their accomplishments since the last meeting. There's almost no way for the CEO to determine if the nonsales teams are overperforming or underperforming.

In her management meeting presentation, the head of Human Resources communicates information like this:

- Five open positions at the start of the month
- Received 500 resumes this month and rejected 300 of them
- Conducted 60 first-round interviews
- Conducted 10 second-round interviews
- Made offers to two candidates
- Filled one open position

All this sounds pretty good to the CEO until he realizes he has no frame of reference. How many interviews *should* have been conducted this month? Is it reasonable that of 500 resumes, only two candidates received offers? How much is this recruiting effort costing? The CEO asks the head of Human Resources a simple question: "Are you satisfied with these results?"

The head of Human Resources proudly proclaims the busyness of the small HR department with its immense recruiting burden. She states that her team cannot continue at this breakneck speed without burning out. Although the CEO is polite, he can't resist asserting that working hard isn't always the same as working smart. He also wishes that Human Resources had established recruiting objectives so he could know if they were meeting them. Instead, Human Resources provided quasi-metrics— information that is numerically based but without enough context to differentiate success from failure.

CEOs Want Numbers

Current-day management theory encourages CEOs to mathematically assess the performance of every nook and cranny of their companies. Hence, CEOs demand metrics for each employee and enter them into spreadsheets. Crunching the numbers allows CEOs to differentiate the workhorses from the slackers.

Jobs that don't require humanity are the easiest to quantify with metrics. For example, one can easily measure an employee in an Amazon fulfillment warehouse by their efficiency in picking items within a time window. The job of an Amazon picker requires no art and no creativity. When the technology exists for nimble robots to pick products, humans in these jobs with their weak backs and bum knees will likely become a quaint artifact of the past.

Jobs requiring humanity are much harder to replace with robots. For example, a therapist who listens to problems and provides insights is much harder to replace with AI. From a business perspective, it's easy enough to measure a therapist's billable hours, new patient acquisition, existing patient retention, and positive Yelp reviews. While these metrics may have some oblique relationship to the therapist's skill, real success in therapy results in patients making positive changes in their lives. Often, successful therapy depends on the serendipitous alchemy of a stellar patient–therapist matchup. Great therapists may help patients so much that they may no longer require therapy.

What about the jobs in a typical company? Are technical geniuses and marketing savants governable by metrics or should these creatives have da Vinci's freedom to do as they please? Any executive responsible for a business's bottom line would argue for metrics. The free spirits who also happen to occupy corporate jobs might argue for artistic freedom. Managers probably prefer a bit more Michelangelo and a bit less da Vinci.

A Compromise: Objectives and Key Results

Establishing objectives with success measures that don't stifle creativity is a reasonable compromise. This is indeed a tall order. Fortunately, Kleiner Perkins venture capital investor John Doerr wrote the book on these types of objectives, called *Objectives and Key Results (OKRs)* (Doerr 2018).

OKRs are the brainchild of the late Andy Grove, Intel's legendary President and CEO. John Doerr worked at Intel before leaving to join Venture Capital powerhouse, Kleiner Perkins. So, Doerr learned OKRs at the feet of the master.

OKRs are a management methodology that helps ensure everyone in a company is focusing their efforts on the same important issues. A person without corporate experience might question why everyone in a company *wouldn't* focus on the same important issues. After all, isn't the point of a company to band together to solve a common set of problems?

Yes, everyone in a company *should* row their oars in the same direction. However, it's a huge challenge, even in small companies, to inculcate a common understanding of the mission. Masochistic CEOs receive rude awakenings after asking employees to provide their understanding of the company's mission. Rather than expressing anger at employees for not *getting it*, these CEOs should first ensure that management has a common understanding. Then, managers should communicate the mission repeatedly until it sticks with all employees.

The *objective* portion of the OKR is easy. The objective is merely *what* is to be achieved. Ideally, objectives are significant, unambiguous, tangible, and possibly audacious. Ideally, objectives provide clarity and leave no room for ambiguity.

The *key results* (KR) portion of the OKRs provides the gates and accounting for *how* the objective will be met. The best KRs are exacting and time-boxed, while also being aggressive yet achievable. Most importantly, KRs are measurable and demonstrable. Key results must contain numbers. This way, the OKRs requirements are met, or they aren't— there's no fuzziness. At the end of a prescribed period, the key result is designated completed or not. When all the key results of an OKR are completed, the OKR is considered achieved.

Two Flavors of OKRs

The point of committed OKRs is to provide a clear path to accomplishing goals. The rigor of the KRs keeps objectives from being spongy and nebulous. With metric-driven KRs, determining successful completion is objective, not subjective. Aspirational OKRs are the second type that guide moonshot-level thinking. The point of creating aspirational OKRs is to think big but think logically. If one creates an audacious goal, some well-considered KRs bring it a bit closer to reality. Even though not all aspirational OKRs will be achieved, there's little chance of accomplishing aspirational goals if they remain in someone's head without the rigor of the OKR process.

The Flavor De Jour in Tech

OKRs are all the rage in tech circles. John Doerr/Kleiner Perkins was an early investor in Google. John Doerr presented OKRs to the original Google team of 30, and they became early adopters. Google still relies on OKRs to keep its business aligned. Google Cofounder and Alphabet CEO, Larry Page, wrote the foreward to Doerr's book. The Bill & Melinda Gates Foundation is also an OKR proponent.

Between Intel, Google, and the Gates Foundation, a person might conclude OKRs are the province of huge organizations. But what about startups? Does the energy and attention required to construct reasonable OKRs outweigh the benefits for small companies? Larry Page would say, *No*, and remind skeptics that Google became Google because it was a startup that adopted OKRs (Doerr 2018, X). Page would probably also admit that OKRs aren't easy. His team coalesced their OKR experiences and published a useful guide to pitfalls to avoid and best practices (Google, "Google's OKR Playbook").

Potential OKR Pitfalls

Some of the following items reflect Google's wisdom about OKRs that can go astray (Google, "Google's OKR Playbook"). Some of these items address common OKR mistakes not identified by Google.

1. **Setting too many, too few, or low-value OKRs**—OKRs aren't a laundry list of tasks that may or may not be completed. The core idea of committed OKRs is that these are must-have items because they provide tremendous business value. Having too many OKRs dilutes their effectiveness. Having too few OKRs suggests the team isn't using its full capacity. Low-value OKRs aren't worth doing.
2. **Status quo OKRs**—There's little point to OKRs that reflect what a team is already doing. The point of OKRs is to recognize changes in the business-as-usual that will bring additional value to customers or to the team.
3. **Confusing key results with tasks**—Key results are the measures that determine the success or failure of the objective. Tasks are items to be

undertaken. The objective of the OKR almost certainly has a set of associated tasks, but these should not be confused with key results.

4. **Setting and forgetting**—OKRs require regular care and feeding. The most effective OKRs occur during a financial quarter and need almost constant monitoring. Since OKRs reflect an organization's most important goals, well-run companies focus on OKRs during management meetings. OKRs should be transparent and visible to everyone across the organization.

5. **Using OKRs to evaluate performance or affect compensation**— Although an employee's effectiveness in completing OKRs should be viewed positively in a performance review, tying OKRs directly to compensation is a huge no-no. If OKRs are used for compensation and advancement, employees will game them to ensure they're easy to accomplish; this is exactly what employees do with story point estimation when management tries to tie them to compensation.

6. **Small-minded aspirational OKRs**—Rather than asking, "What could we do if we hire a few additional employees?" it's better to ask, "What could we do that would rock our customers' worlds?" Stating an audacious goal is the first step in achieving it. If the business rallies around the goal, one of the KRs might be to hire additional people.

7. **Sandbagging**—A team's committed OKRs should consume all its available people. A team's committed and aspirational OKRs should consume slightly more than its available people. If the sum of a team's OKRs can be completed without utilizing everyone, it's a sign that the team isn't pushing hard enough or is over-resourced.

8. **Setting nonmeasurable key results**—Although it's easy to understand that KRs should be numeric, producing these numbers takes some work. Conceiving non-numeric KRs is a temptation that shouldn't be permitted because these kinds of KRs can't be measured. For example, if the objective is to make a web page's interface more intuitive, the KR, "Everyone agrees the page is easier to use," is unacceptable. Instead, a KR like, "Measure the time of data entry with 100 users and achieve 10 percent faster completion than before," is acceptable.

OKR Example and Counterexample

Discussing the concept of OKRs is simple, but constructing great OKRs is deceptively difficult. The following examples present two OKRs, one bad and one good.

Example OKR:
Objective: Improve the website
Key Result 1: Produce more engaging content.
Key Result 2: Beef up the website design.
Key Result 3: Poll employees to determine if the website improves significantly.

This OKR is nebulous and unacceptable. Improving the website is subjective, meaning different things to different people. Subjective objectives are immeasurable. The first two key results are tasks, not measurable results. Ideally, these first two tasks are required to achieve numeric key results. The third key result suggests a numeric measure, but it's measuring opinions, not an actual improvement.

Counterexample OKR:
Objective: Increase website engagement
Key Result 1: Ensure we get at least 1,000 pageviews from SEO efforts by end of Q1.
Key Result 2: Decrease bounce rate from 75 percent to 50 percent by end of Q1.
Key Result 3: Increase average pages per visit from 1 to 2.5 by end of Q1.

This OKR introduces a few webby concepts that bear definition:

SEO—Search engine optimization is the process used to optimize a website's technical configuration. SEO enables a website's pages to become easily findable and higher ranked by search engines.
Bounce rate—The bounce rate measures the percentage of people who land on a website, don't interact, and leave. Website designers work to reduce bounce rates.

Average pages per visit—The number of pages website visitors click on is an excellent measure of the site's engagement. Increasing pages per visit reflects more interesting and engaging content.

This website engagement OKR hits all the high points of a great OKR:

1. The objective is clear.
2. The KRs are measurable and time-bound.
3. The goals of this OKR are ambitious but achievable.
4. The business will benefit significantly from successfully completing this OKR.

Case Study: Customer Retention and OKRs

A vacationing CEO sits on the beach watching his grandchildren build a sandcastle as he ruminates about his Q4 corporate objectives. One grandchild runs into the water to fill her pail with water to dribble onto the sandcastle. By the time she fills the bucket and reaches the sandcastle, the bucket is empty. The bucket has a hole. Before she notices the leak, the girl runs back to the water and refills the bucket to no avail—it's still empty by the time she reaches the sandcastle. Eventually, the girl notices the leak, refills the bucket, and sticks her finger in the hole. Some water is lost, but enough remains to tend to the sandcastle.

The CEO views the leaky bucket as a metaphor for his company. The company has lost several important customers over the past year. His small sales team is hitting its targets reeling in new customers. However, the new sales revenue isn't replacing the revenue from the lost customers.

The CEO knows it typically costs five times more to acquire new customers than retain existing ones. The company's customer base churn is like his granddaughter's leaky bucket. She can run herself ragged refilling the bucket, but until she plugs the leak, she cannot progress forward. The CEO decides his objective is to stop the leaks.

When he gathers his grandchildren and heads back to their beach house, the CEO scrawls the following objective on the back of a takeout menu:

Find a way to eliminate the loss of our lucrative existing customers because new customers are so expensive to acquire.

As he tries to produce KRs to measure the objective, the CEO considers why the company is experiencing churn. It doesn't take him long to produce a list.

1. Sales is heavily incentivized to make new sales. Upselling to current customers isn't as well compensated. Therefore, his Sales team focuses more on new sales than tending to current customers.

2. The company's competitors are going to market with whiz-bang new features much faster than his company is releasing similar functionality. Customers have complained and left because the company isn't keeping up with its competitors. Customers explained they're willing to be patient if they know the features are imminent. However, customers also grouse they lack visibility into the company's roadmap.

3. The company is frequently blindsided. When the CEO asks why they are leaving, customers often cite problems never communicated to the Customer Success team.

After a bit more thought, the CEO writes the following OKR:

Objective: Reduce customer churn to *zero*

   Key Result 1: Ensure that Sales visits every customer at least once a quarter starting at the beginning of Q4.

   Key Result 2: Release new software to customers every three weeks instead of the current quarterly releases. By cutting the time from three months to three weeks, finished features will get to customers faster.

   Key Result 3: Customer Support ensures it will speak to all customers monthly and solicit at least three problems or needs from each conversation.

The CEO is proud of himself. He's trying to shake things up and believes bringing OKRs to his company will force better alignment between departments. While babysitting his grandchildren, he has produced what he considers a solid OKR and sees it cascading to Sales, Engineering, and Customer support.

More specifically, the CEO expects to give Sales his first key result, which they will use as the objective of their OKR. The head of Sales will make her own key results, which will become objectives for the people on her team. The same will occur with key results for the Engineering and Customer Success teams. He envisions a broad, leafy family tree-like structure that starts with his OKR. Each management level inherits from the level above. With this approach, OKRs will be fully aligned all the way down to the nonmanagerial employee level.

The CEO can't wait to return to work and explain this top-down approach to OKRs.

The Phony Lure of Cascading Objectives

When the CEO returns to the office after his vacation, he gathers the management team and explains his beach babysitting revelation. A few of his longtime managers surreptitiously roll their eyes at one another. They're accustomed to their boss returning from *vacation* with new work for all of them. One employee mutters to another, "I'm surprised his kids trust him with the grandchildren when he's always distracted thinking about business."

As the CEO explains his idea of top-down, cascading OKRs, he receives gentle pushback from some managers and open hostility from others. One of the managers with deep OKR experience makes three points:

1. The CEO should provide vision and direction to the company, but he must leave it to his Management team to figure out for themselves how their teams should best add value. That is, the CEO's objectives are welcome and expected, but he may not dictate his managers' objectives from his key results.

2. Constructing significant, measurable OKRs is difficult, even for people who have done it before. A top-down approach where each rung on the reporting ladder inherits its objectives from the higher level becomes chaotic when key results change at the highest level. And

changing key results to make stronger, more measurable OKRs is more the rule than the exception.

3. Adopting a balanced approach of top-down and bottom-up is far preferable when it comes to setting OKRs. Many of the best ideas come from nonmanagerial employees who have their own understanding of business needs and priorities. OKRs will fail in the company unless they are a collaborative process.

The manager with the OKR experience in the previous paragraph speaks the truth. While it's possible to implement top-down OKRs, this approach ignores the valuable insights of the people who perform the work. CEOs and others in the C-suite should provide vision and strategy. If the rest of the company understands the vision and strategy, they are better equipped to intelligently execute.

Back to the vacationing CEO. He is accustomed to being the smartest guy in the room and bristles at the pushback. However, he handpicked his management team because of their experience and intelligence. Although he believes he's correct that his top-down OKRs are the perfect way to align the company, he's willing to allow his team to further explain themselves.

The outspoken VP of Engineering offers additional detail about the shortcomings of top-down OKRs. He begins, "I understand you're trying to plug the leaks, but not only is it offensive to dictate that it's my team's contribution to release software every three weeks, but it's short-sighted." He goes on to suggest these two objectives:

1. *Put new software features in front of customers as soon as they're ready.* The VP of Engineering explains that the CEO's *three-week release* objective isn't ambitious enough. The Engineering team wants to explore *continuous delivery*, a process that enables immediate deployments to production environments, to deliver software quickly, and to solicit immediate customer feedback. Using this approach, software could be released daily or multiple times daily.

2. *Offer customers a strategic, outcome-driven roadmap that clearly outlines the company's goals without committing to specific dates for features.* The VP of Engineering is aware of the disconnect between customer

expectations and engineering plans. Since the CEO hadn't addressed this disconnect in his objective, this second objective fills the gap.

The CEO silently congratulates himself for hiring managers who aren't *yes people*. He understands how the VP of Engineering absorbed the big idea of stopping customer churn and produced a significantly more impressive objective. Furthermore, the second objective is important to keep customers informed about the company's plans without promising specific dates.

The other department managers mimic the VP of Engineering for their own disciplines. The VP of Sales explains that the CEO's objective for sales of *visiting customers every quarter* doesn't adequately prevent customer churn. The Sales team must change its compensation structure to treat current customers as precious commodities and take responsibility for retaining them. The VP of Sales suggests a broader objective like, "Grow revenue from existing customers while continuing to win new customers." She then tosses out a few key results, including customer visits and stronger collaboration with Customer Success.

The CEO is astonished that the department managers produced more ambitious objectives than he imagined. After providing the vision, the CEO starts the ball rolling and wisely decides to get out of the way.

If OKRs are constructed thoughtfully and executed well, they benefit the company. The transparency of OKRs enables all employees to understand why their work is vital to the company. The cross-team connective tissue that frequently frays as companies grow can be mended with OKRs. If a Management team focuses on successfully completing committed OKRs, they can band together to focus on and ensure the success of OKRs in jeopardy. OKRs are the metrics senior managers want, enabling them to focus on the big picture without resorting to internal metrics, like story points, to judge progress.

OKRs Versus Management by Objectives

Peter Drucker introduced his theory of *management by objectives* (MBO), a goal-setting framework, in his 1954 book, *Practice of Management* (Drucker 1954).

MBO is a management system where managers and employees collaborate to develop areas of responsibility for employees. Standards are established and metrics are used to determine employees' performance. The underlying belief of MBO is that employees perform better if they understand what's expected of them. Employee participation in the MBO goal-setting process fosters loyalty and dedication while also aligning objectives across organizations.

MBO sure sounds like OKR. Are OKRs merely a colorized, weak remake of a successful, old movie designed to appeal to a younger audience? Actually, no. MBO and OKR have some significant differences outlined in the following table.

Table 6.1 MBO versus OKR

	MBO	**OKR**
Origination	Peter Drucker in 1954	Andy Grove in the 1970s
Frequency of review	Reviewed yearly—objectives set for the entire year and analyzed at an employee's annual performance review.	Higher frequency of review. OKRs are generally set for a month or quarter and frequently reviewed to make course corrections.
Visibility	Strictly confidential between a manager and an employee.	Completely transparent. The power of OKRs is that they are publicly shared.
Purpose	Used to determine compensation and possibly bonus during an annual review.	Compensation remains unaffected by the level of achievement. The focus of OKRs is to push the boundaries to achieve excellence.
Definition of success	Since compensation is directly related to the fulfillment of objectives, employees are expected to achieve 100%. Any less and compensation will be lowered.	An average of 60% to 70% achievement is expected. 100% achievement means employees are just playing in their comfort zones. Goals should be ambitious but realistic.

Key Takeaways

1. Story point estimation is the Agile Scrum approach to sizing work items relative to one another.
2. The story point completion achieved by teams, also known as *velocity*, is an internal metric.

3. Upper management's use of story points to measure the effectiveness of teams and individual employees isn't a fair means of evaluation.

4. Upper management might cling to story points as a measure because team managers don't provide any other useful metrics.

5. Current-day management theory encourages the quantitative measurement of companies, teams, and employees.

6. OKRs represent a compromise between quantitative measurement and creativity-stifling metrics.

7. OKRs must be significant, unambiguous, and measurable.

8. There are two flavors of OKRs: committed must-do OKRs and aspirational OKRs.

9. The key results part of OKRs must be numeric.

10. OKRs represent an improvement on the original concept of MBO.

CHAPTER 7

Implementing Organizational Change

Agile isn't magic. Becoming an Agile organization requires each team to build processes for internal and inter-team communication and develop ways to recognize success. Often a gimlet-eyed outsider is the best person to provide a dispassionate assessment and execute changes.

Before even considering bringing in an outsider to solve internal issues, most cost-conscious CEOs prefer a solution from the people already on the payroll. Before seeking solutions, a CEO must articulate the problems. No company, even the most respected and valuable enterprise, is without problems. However, not all problems are created equal.

If a company with a competent management team consistently misses its goals, it's important to determine the root causes. Companies that shoot for the moon may be aiming too high. Organizations with more modest goals that never reach them are the ones that should ask why.

Companies fail for myriad reasons. Some startups never find a market fit for their products and don't pivot to meet market demand. That is, companies that doggedly build products no one is willing to buy are doomed to fail. Other companies fail for more subtle reasons. For example, companies in crowded business verticals must have good products and be sufficiently differentiated from competitors.

When a Company Reaches a Plateau

One of the most vexing problems is when a company plateaus. Sometimes it plays out like this: A company has acquired a set of loyal customers who love the product. The company succeeds enough to grow, either from profits or additional investment.

When the company cannot reach the next level of growth, it's likely because what worked when the company was small no longer works with an expanded team. The tight coupling of teams in a startup almost guarantees that nothing gets dropped on the floor when handing off work between teams. Company growth frays the connective tissue that exists between its teams.

Companies in startup mode adopt a *we wear many hats* approach. An employee hired to write technical documentation may pitch in to test the application. A customer service representative may build the company's website. The idea of wearing many hats is a euphemism for doing whatever's necessary for the company's success, regardless of the reporting structure.

Early-stage company employees thrive on the uncertainty, and sometimes the insanity, of what the day holds. Startups can be chaotic, attracting people who love to swim in these choppy waters. When a company succeeds largely because of the energy of its early-stage employees, continued success requires a different set of behaviors.

Process and best practices are secondary concerns when an early-stage company tries to stay afloat. During a startup's survival phase, employees may proudly tout its flat organizational structure and lack of bureaucratic constraints. A startup team may believe they're following Agile practices, but pivoting a startup is frequently haphazard, not intentional.

A company is forced to mature as it grows. A startup's "wear many hats" mentality is no longer a prized trait. Instead, employees in growth companies learn to stay in their lanes and hew to the responsibilities of their positions. When the willingness to work across teams for the common good becomes suspect instead of rewarded, additional processes are required to ensure that the benefits of startup cohesion remain, albeit in a more organized manner.

Companies that don't execute the organizational changes required to grow will increase in size without maturing. That is, they become big babies. Nostalgically relying on the disorganization of the startup days, instead of introducing new processes, causes companies to flounder. Startups can't scale without *some* additional bureaucracy and management structure. Early employees who dislike the constraints of a growing company may be happier joining another startup.

Opportunities at Inflection Points

Like a gangly teenager, companies go through awkward transitions as they fill out. Interestingly, the especially awkward moments in a company provide the most significant opportunities to grow. For example, a company that receives an investment injection may now hire for the positions that were previously shared responsibilities among the startup team.

Before even publishing descriptions for these new positions, thoughtful leaders may carefully consider the skill sets required for the company's future success that the current team lacks. However, identifying the missing pieces when hiring additional staff requires both a frank assessment of the current team's shortcomings and a clear understanding of what it takes to reach the next level of success.

In more concrete terms, the following real-world opportunities are typically considered as companies grow. Note that this list is merely a set of general growth-oriented questions. The answers to these questions depend on a company's business circumstances.

1. **Sales**—Should the company hire additional salespeople and continue a direct sales strategy or implement a channel strategy where third parties such as partners, distributors, or value-added resellers sell the company's products? A channel strategy puts more *boots on the ground* but also requires product maturity, including seamless deployment, clear documentation, and third-party training.

2. **HR**—The conundrum of growing companies is teams that most need to hire additional workers are too busy to recruit. Should HR take an active role in building a recruiting program, or should hiring managers continue to shoulder the responsibility for hiring through outsourced recruiters? A strong HR leader will insist on uniformity and fairness in hiring across teams.

3. **Quality assurance**—When is the right time to transition from a manual testing organization to automated testing? When a company's products mature and user interfaces stabilize, it's time to consider an automation framework and transition manual smoke tests to automated scripts.

4. **Operations**—Should Operations migrate from a hosting center to a cloud provider? Is now the right time to build automation scripts that make deployments a pushbutton operation? How about building a deployment *pipeline* that automatically runs tests and deploys whenever new software is committed to a version control system? In most companies, Operations is a growth area that requires strong, experienced leadership.

5. **Engineering**—Should Engineering adopt new practices like test-driven development that require unit tests to accompany any new code? Is now the time to consider refactoring or rearchitecture projects? With a growing team, is it time to break a monolithic product into individually deployable micro-services?

6. **Product management**—When should Product Management transition from a seat-of-the-pants operation to a more data-driven organization? Is now the time to hire a full-time user experience designer instead of continuing to outsource the work? Finding product–market fit is hard enough in a startup, but lucky or thoughtful leaders can make it past the startup phase. Making real headway post-startup requires Product Management to grow up.

Four Keys: Recognizing Corporate Agile Readiness

Acknowledging that a *business as usual approach* isn't cutting it is the first step in retooling a company for agility. The second step to corporate agility is committing to change. However, making changes without well-defined reasoning is merely making change for the sake of change. *Different* isn't always better.

These four keys to recognizing corporate Agile readiness constitute a roadmap for determining the best ways to grow and implement processes to achieve objectives.

Key 1: Dispassionate Agility Assessment

Each department in a company serves an essential purpose. If a department isn't pulling its load, it's a drag on the entire business. Although departmental problems affect business outcomes, determining the cause of the problems is seldom straightforward.

Here's one of the most common business squabbles occurs between Sales and Engineering:

Engineering—"Sales goes out of their way to sell products we haven't built. They should become more knowledgeable about the products we *do have*, sell these products, and stop selling vaporware."

Sales—"We keenly understand the company's products. The problem is that customers don't want our current products. If Engineering built what customers need, we wouldn't have to get so creative in the sales process."

Who's right and who's wrong in the engineering/sales argument? Companies that achieve product–market fit don't have these problems. If products are built to address market needs, customers clamor for the software and Sales isn't forced to sell vaporware. Sales is in the wrong if products fit the market and Sales peddles products that don't exist. Engineering is in the wrong if its products don't appeal to the company's target customers.

Like many corporate disagreements, determining the responsible party is seldom black and white. There's almost always plenty of blame to spread around because no team is ever perfect. The acknowledgment of imperfection opens the door to change.

Instead of becoming embroiled in the internecine conflict between departments, assessing a department in isolation provides a better window into its function or dysfunction. The following types of questions bring transparency to the workings of a department:

1. Does the team produce tangible results at a regular cadence?
2. Does the team have lengthy planning cycles resulting in voluminous documentation?
3. Does the team consistently meet its objectives and deadlines?
4. Does the team believe it's operating well and sees no need to change course?
5. Does the team have processes it follows to manage their work?

Even though these five questions may be answered with a simple Yes or No, a defensive manager would probably pick apart the questions and find a way to paint their team positively. Without any firm way of measuring productivity, much of the assessment amounts to hearsay.

Any assessment of a team requires some triangulation and digging. In the absence of metrics, interviewing the recipients of the team's work products offers a window into the team's effectiveness. Additionally, canvassing other teams' manager's opinions is valuable if the interviewer knows enough to separate facts from politics.

Teams that insist they're well-oiled machines without making changes almost always need interventions. Hubris is one of the deadly sins of a team that prevents its growth. Managers and workers with the humility to acknowledge their imperfections are eager to try new approaches that promise greater success.

Key 2: Establishing a Structure to Measure Success

The previous chapter took a deep dive into metrics and OKRs. It's nearly impossible to assess the effectiveness of a team without metrics. In the previous section, without metrics, the five Yes/No questions may be finessed to paint the respondent in the best light. With metrics, the answers become more definitive with numeric measures to remove the fuzziness of the answers.

The only hope in Key 1 of being dispassionate in assessing agility is to implement the measurement structure of Key 2. The subjective analysis that metrics provide supports assessing teams without emotion or bias.

Even if the five questions expose some weaknesses, having metrics in place suggests the team cares about accountability and improvement. Furthermore, even if the team isn't pressed by management for success statistics, having metrics supports internal assessments of successes and failures.

Organizations that push back against metrics may fear the cold calculus of quantifiable results. Metric avoidance enables managers to claim work product successes that might be considered failures when quantitively evaluated.

Conversely, companies that commit to metric-driven objectives take a leap of faith. No longer will they be given participation trophies for simply putting in the hours. Metrics don't care about effort, attitude, or crazy work hours unless these factors contribute to teams completing their work. Metrics measure results. By creating objectives with measurable results around the critical work, teams learn to ignore noncritical work. Instead of spending long days and weekends focusing on too many tasks, teams work smarter by narrowing their focus. Objectives help teams focus on just the critical work and allow them to defer noncritical work.

Transparent objectives enable management teams to restructure their weekly meetings. The discussion in these meetings centers around the steps a team will take each week to achieve its objectives.

Companies willing to incorporate metrics are good bets to bring agility into their organizations.

Key 3: A Framework for Inter-Team Communication

The human body is marvelously complex. Although each organ has its own specific role, the systems work collaboratively to keep the body healthy. For example, the respiratory and circulatory systems collaborate to oxygenate the body and to eliminate the body of carbon dioxide. The lungs enable oxygen to reach the blood and remove carbon dioxide.

The individual departments in a company function like organs in the human body. Each department has individual responsibilities and objectives. However, company departments don't exist in isolation. They must work together to achieve the greater goals of the company. Like the human body's respiratory and circulatory systems, the Engineering, Product Management, and Marketing teams must collaborate to deliver stellar solutions, educate customers, and inform them about impending product releases. Product releases require exquisite cooperation between teams. Although not as complex as interactions between human organs, successful departmental teamwork similarly begets corporate health.

How do busy departments with separate missions stay aligned? First, each department head must buy into the importance of inter-team alignment. Second, designated individuals from each team must take responsibility for the interaction between their team and other teams. Third, the judicious use of tools enables teams to collaborate without being joined at the hip.

Although meetings to ensure alignment may be necessary, they should be an adjunct to processes and tools, not a replacement. As a rule, companies are best served by avoiding all but essential meetings. Putting processes in place helps to minimize status meetings and other information exchange meetings.

Key 4: Culture of Learning

All the processes, measurement, communication between teams, and Agile readiness don't amount to anything if a company doesn't fully understand its customers' most pressing problems. Furthermore, understanding customers' problems is useless unless solid plans for solving them accompany it.

What does it mean to fully understand a customer's most pressing problems? Gaining a full understanding of a problem requires understanding the problem and its underlying causes. Customers are willing to pay big bucks for products that alleviate their most acute suffering. Customers are less willing to purchase solutions for secondary problems.

The following case study illustrates the importance of digging deep to understand a problem. On the surface, many problems seem simple and it takes effort to uncover complexities.

Case Study: Fully Understanding a Customer's Problem

Remember the Burger Shack from the beginning of the book? If not, that's okay because this case study stands alone.

Initially, the Burger Shack only served finely crafted hamburgers with locally sourced beef. Customers clamored for fries to go with their burgers. The surfer buddies/burger moguls decided to offer hand-cut fries. They invested in the deep fryers and spent months perfecting their technique. The Burger Shack serves one size of hand-cut fries—a generous helping that's large enough for two people to share. They succeeded in spades. The reviewers gush as much about the hand-cut fries as the burgers.

The Burger Shack runs out of hand-cut fries when the lunch rush is especially heavy. Disappointed customers grumble, vowing to arrive earlier the next time.

If the solution to the shortage was merely to cook more fries, the problem could be easily resolved. Unfortunately, the problem is much more complicated. So complicated, in fact, that the owners hired a consultant to help solve the problem.

The deliciousness of Burger Shack hand-cut fries doesn't come cheap. Preparing the Russet potatoes is a multistep process for two employees that begins the night before at each store (they expanded to three additional locations from their original shack at the beach).

The hand-cut fry preparation process includes peeling, cutting, rinsing, refrigerating, and blanching the potatoes. None of the steps is optional in the exacting process. Refrigeration is the problem.

With everything else that must be refrigerated, fitting in the vats of cut potatoes is like a game of Jenga. Storing additional vats of potatoes isn't possible without purchasing additional refrigerators. None of the kitchens in the three locations can accommodate additional refrigerators without reconfiguring the setup and reducing the workspace.

The consultant considers multiple solutions:

1. Reduce the portion size so the restaurant doesn't run out during a heavy rush of business.
2. Fill in with frozen fries when the restaurant runs out of fries.
3. Determine the soundness of investing in reconfiguring the kitchen and adding additional refrigeration.
4. Weigh the costs in #3 against leasing additional refrigeration space in an offsite location. This requires transporting the potatoes to the stores, which must be considered in the cost analysis.
5. Consolidate all hand-cut fry preparation to a separate location. Not only does this solution require transporting the fries, but it also requires additional employees for the massive operation.

The point of this scenario isn't to debate the possible solutions (although the owners chose the stopgap #1 solution and it's worked out well) but to illustrate how problems must be deeply understood before it's possible to devise viable solutions.

Paradoxically, the final and most important pillar of retooling a company for agility is culture, not process, skill, communication, measurement, or operational excellence. Companies that never find a product–market fit often suffer from hubris. Executives who have experienced previous successful professional endeavors are most susceptible to excessive confidence. The attitude that, "We don't need to ask the customer what they need because we already know," is a recipe for the company's untimely death. Even when all the signs point to a product that won't gain market traction, know-it-all management doggedly refuses to pivot.

A learning culture is about more than employees' desire to learn new programming languages or accounting techniques. Companies hungry for knowledge are innately curious. Curiosity leads employees to dig below the surface of their customers' problems. Knowing the *what* is the basis for understanding customers' problems. Curiosity causes a team to learn why the problem exists and persist in gaining a well-rounded understanding. Once a team fully understands the contours of customer problems, only then are they positioned to propose solutions.

Multidisciplinary discovery teams are the byproduct of a curiosity culture. Instead of a single Product Manager deciding how to craft a solution, a team of experts across a company craft approaches that fully address the problem in a technically feasible and elegant manner. Although a great Product Manager may be adept at scoping a well-fitting solution, having design, engineering, and quality experts viewing the problem through their unique lenses invariably results in stronger outcomes.

Most Companies Require Outside Assistance

Recognizing corporate dysfunction doesn't require an expert. It isn't rocket science. Missed sales targets, customer churn, disappointing usage statistics, and negative customer feedback are the in-one's-face indicators of problems.

Companies, even small ones, are like ocean liners. Small changes in direction are relatively simple, but sharp turns to avoid calamities cause the dining room glassware to break and shake up the passengers.

Furthermore, avoiding icebergs requires someone to look out for them and quickly communicate the danger.

A CEO may recognize the dangers the company faces but not understand their severity. Therefore, the CEOs may give the Management team mixed messages to fix the problems ASAP without a timeline or direction.

Typically, department managers are inundated with deadlines. Unless the CEO provides actionable direction, busy managers will likely back-burner the directive until they have time to determine the best course of action. Consequently, managers may acknowledge the problems but postpone devising solutions until the next deadline is met. And when another deadline follows on the heels of the previous one, managers pay lip service to making significant changes. Becoming mired in the tactical concerns of the day-to-day grind prevents managers from taking a longer-term view. However, the manager's job is to think strategically even if intensive daily demands force them to act tactically.

Experienced outsiders add value in situations where managers are busy, threats are present, and solutions are ill-formed. Consultants aren't necessarily smarter or more insightful than the company's employees. The benefit consultants bring is their disconnection from the day-to-day concerns that prevent higher-level thinking. Consequently, consultants are well-positioned to understand a CEO's concerns. If a consultant is experienced, they will also devise achievable and measurable solutions to the problems.

Consultants face justifiable wariness from managers who don't want to be told how to do their jobs. Managers may argue that the consultants' superficial understanding of the company will result in half-baked solutions that won't solve real problems.

Exasperated CEOs likely also consider consultants a last resort. If a CEO has alerted managers to the problems and they don't take the bait, continuing business as usual, the sudden appearance of consultants may feel like punishment.

Instead of viewing outside opinions as a last resort, proactive CEOs recognize the value of these opinions and seek them before the company reaches the crisis stage.

The following indicators give proactive CEOs a rationale to seek outside opinions.

Ignoring Strategy in Favor of Day-to-Day Tactical Concerns

The pressures of deadlines, customer demands, and fires sometimes require pragmatic decision-making that contradicts overall corporate strategy. When managers keep their heads in the weeds too long, it's easy to forget about the big picture and adopt a day-to-day viewpoint. When the volume of shortsighted decisions begins to jeopardize achieving greater objectives, it's time for a reckoning.

Managerial Squabbles

When everything's going swimmingly in a company, its managers typically live harmoniously. Even then, the occasional scuffle between teams is more the rule than the exception. When managers wage constant and unrelenting battles, it's a good indicator of problems that aren't resolved successfully.

Customer Discontent and Churn

Discontented, grumpy customers aren't necessarily a problem. Paradoxically, customers who are passionate about a company's products are the ones who heap criticism. Ignoring customer discontent, however, is unwise. What begins as criticism may morph into rage if customers feel unheard. The departure of loyal customers is a solid indicator that the company either doesn't know how to allay customer concerns or doesn't care about them.

Employee Attrition

Some employee attrition is normal. In the best case, employees run to new opportunities affording professional and personal growth. If Glassdoor reviews indicate employees are *running from* the company, or if the company is experiencing unusually high levels of attrition, it's another indicator of problems. Employee discontent is a pernicious and contagious problem that may have devastating consequences if not understood and rectified.

Employees Uninformed About Company Direction

When a CEO quizzes employees about the company's mission and direction and there are more Fs than As, either the company lacks an underlying strategy, or its managers are doing a poor job communicating. In either case, when employees don't understand why they're coming to work every day, they may find new jobs where they feel they're making a difference.

Missed Deadlines

Consistently missed deadlines points to poor planning, poor execution, or poor processes. All the other items in this list are potential consequences of continuously missing deadlines. An outsider's input is warranted if a company lacks a realistic plan for meeting its deadlines.

Missed Sales Targets

Sales is traditionally the only company department with measurable results. The revolving door of Sales jettisons managers and employees who miss their sales targets and brings in new employees who promise to do better. Presumably, the company doesn't hire incompetent salespeople. Sales targets may be missed for various reasons that have nothing to do with the salespeople's ability. Instead of eliminating underperforming salespeople and insisting new blood will solve all the problems, it's wiser to dig deeper.

The aforementioned red flags have root causes that cut across the entire company. Missed sales targets are typically blamed on salespeople, but product deficiencies, poor customer support, and unclear communications are often contributing factors. While it's possible to address these problems in-house, it requires the cooperation and teamwork of managers who are already facing stressful situations. A Management team may embark upon self-improvement projects with a good attitude, but it often results in finger-pointing and turf battles. An overseer perceived by managers as unbiased has more latitude to effect changes that would be resisted if suggested by peers.

Selecting a Consultant

Not all consultants are created equal, but nearly all their work boils down to the following three categories. Engagements may necessitate finding consultants with strengths in some or all these categories.

1. **Providing functional expertise**—These are the *been there, have the scars to prove it* consultants who can roll up their sleeves and pitch in. The role of a consultant with functional expertise is typically to put processes in place and coach/mentor frontline employees about the implementation. The consultant can perform the work themself, but this isn't generally the best use of consulting dollars. The goal is to enable success with the current team in the future absence of the consultant.

2. **Providing an objective analysis**—A knowledgeable consultant provides an objective opinion if a company has a major decision. Although the company's principals have a greater understanding of the business domain, they may also have biases and blind spots. A consultant with no political agenda or operational baggage can provide a fresh, unbiased opinion. Sometimes when a team is dead-locked over a decision, another voice in the mix breaks the logjam.

3. **Providing outsourced brain power**—When corporate decision-makers are mired in deadlines and urgent projects, they are too busy to devote the required brain power to hard problems. In these cases, the consultant acts as a brain for hire. The consultant must be savvy enough to learn about the business to suggest pertinent solutions. This category of consulting is the most resented by management. Consultants become targets when they are brought in to provide solutions that employees are too busy to give. Common criticisms of these consultants are of the ilk, "It's easy to make pronouncements when they have no skin in the game and are leaving it to the rest of us to implement these grand ideas," or "They don't understand the business well enough to back up these recommendations, which will not work." The best way to counter employee criticism is to give the consultant time and materials to learn so they gain credibility from employees. Additionally, empower the consultant to collaborate with employees to craft achievable solutions.

Checklist: General Questions for Choosing a Consultant

The following table addresses a variety of considerations when hiring a consultant.

Table 7.1 Considerations for hiring a consultant

Questions	Yes	No	Considerations
Do we need a consultant?			This is often the most vexing of the questions about consultants. Managers may push back against bringing in outsiders, but a CEO sometimes overrules them. Longstanding, acknowledged unresolved problems may require a consultant with fresh ideas and an unbiased perspective to break the logjam.
Are we willing to make changes?			This is a tricky one. Often, an exasperated CEO brings in a consultant to shake things up. Unless there's buy-in from the management team, it's difficult for top-down edicts to take root. Before hiring a consultant, ensure the entire team recognizes the need for change and find someone who will work well with the team.
Are we willing to manage this consulting engagement?			No matter how senior, any third party requires oversight to remove obstacles and keep the engagement on track. Typically, companies that hire consultants have the best outcomes when the engagement is treated as a partnership. This implies that in addition to the cost of the consulting agreement, managerial time devoted to the project should be considered an additional cost of the engagement.
Does this engagement require industry expertise?			Some consulting engagements require intimate industry knowledge, and paying a consultant to learn is not cost efficient. In this case, finding an industry expert and expecting a greater hourly fee is better.
Do we have clear expectations for what we expect a consultant to accomplish?			If the answer is *No*, seek a consultant to assess your business problems and provide ideas about the best path forward. When a consultant makes suggestions, arriving at a final plan is a collaborative process.
Do we seek the implementation of ideas or just the ideas?			This one reflects the difference between consultants with ideas versus consultants willing to roll up their sleeves and work with the team to implement the ideas. Many consultants do both.

(Continues)

(*Continued*)

Questions	Yes	No	Considerations
Do we need coaching and/or mentoring?			Consultants who work with front-line employees can build processes that persist beyond the consulting engagement. If one of the goals of the consulting engagement is to grow the team, choose a consultant with the people skills to engage and encourage employees.
Do we expect the consultant to work with our customers or is this an internal engagement?			If the consultant will speak directly with customers, choose carefully. Consultants who represent the company professionally and knowledgeably must already possess industry expertise. Hiring an industry insider is typically more expensive than a generalist who learns enough to complete a project. If the primary aspects of the project do not require industry expertise, it's more cost-effective to hire a consultant who works behind the scenes, letting employees handle direct customer interactions.
Can the consultant help us discover our mission and establish a strategy?			A high-end consultant can help position a company and assist in defining its core competencies. This level of advice requires experience and a willingness to learn the particulars of what makes each company unique.
Do we want the consultant to inject cultural change?			Changing an organization's culture requires a mix of qualitative and quantitative skills and soft skills. Additionally, an experienced consultant helps align culture with strategy and company structure.

Ideal Consultant Characteristics

The preceding checklist suggests that different circumstances require different kinds of consultants. That said, these are the common denominators of all successful consultants:

1. **Experience**—Even if a consultant is inexperienced in a particular business domain, they should have the background to be a quick study. Hiring consultants with a wide variety of business experience is especially useful when the engagement goals are ill-defined and established through consultant–employer collaboration.
2. **Openness**—Consulting is about collaboration. Even if a consultant is whispering sweet nothings about business improvement into the

CEO's ear, the consultant will speak with others in the company to form opinions. Consultants who explain why they're asking questions and bring employees into the process are typically successful.

3. **Positivity**—Companies engage consultants to solve some gnarly and unpleasant problems. Consultants who are excited about finding solutions that work for the team radiate infectious enthusiasm.

4. **Curiosity**—Interested in understanding what make a company unique and what it does better than any other companies.

Consultant Follow-On Support

Most consulting engagements are impermanent, often with a predefined end date. Consultants will structure their approach in preparation for their departure when the team must stand alone. This means that even when consultants roll up their sleeves to execute changes, they are careful to use it as a teaching experience rather than doing it themselves. One sign of an effective consultant is one who is no longer needed when the engagement ends.

Invariably, the team will need guidance and direction after a consultant departs. Establishing a small tranche of follow-on hours for a consultant to gradually step away helps to ease the transition.

Occasionally, if a team takes ownership of a consultant-inspired process, training the staff is necessary. In many cases, the teams have adopted the process so fully that they're also capable trainers. If not, any consultant should be pleased to offer training provided hours are set aside for the follow-on engagement.

Managing Consultants

Even the highest-end consultant requires oversight and support. Regardless of a consultant's business expertise, they aren't expert in every business. Applying a one-size-fits-all recipe for success without understanding which ingredients to alter constitutes a failed consulting engagement. To add true value, consultants must dig in and learn everything they can about their employer. Anything the company can do to facilitate this learning helps to guarantee a successful consulting arrangement.

The Hidden Costs of Consulting

Aside from the cost of hiring a consultant, corporate accountants may not consider the management overhead that's also required. No competent consultant needs to be bossed around, but they do require a sounding board for ideas, an offensive lineman to clear the way for the consultant to learn, and someone to hold them to task; the *sponsor* typically occupies all of these roles, and it takes time. Although a manager's time is already accounted for in the payroll, there's no additional cost for a manager to sponsor a consultant. However, the lost opportunity cost of what a manager cannot accomplish because of consultant management should be considered in the cost calculus of a consulting engagement.

Structuring a Consulting Engagement

In many cases, the deliverables of a consulting engagement are clear and agreed upon upfront. For example, if a consultant is building the company a new data warehouse, it's relatively easy to outline the steps in a statement of work (SOW). When an engagement is less well-defined, like being employed to fix whatever's most broken, it's typically up to the consultant to take some time to learn enough to make a proposal. No work should start in earnest until the consultant and sponsor agree upon the focus, milestones, deliverables, and the timeline. Finally, the consultant must commit this agreement to a written SOW.

In general, consulting engagements are best executed as Agile projects. This way, it's easier to focus on individual milestones and deliverables, assessing success or failure. Furthermore, if the project goes sideways with unexpected obstacles, the iterative work renders an end-of-sprint course correction much easier.

If a consulting arrangement isn't run in an Agile fashion, keeping the engagement short achieves the same results. A short SOW forces an evaluation at the end when the sponsor decides the necessity of commissioning follow-on work.

A poorly structured consulting engagement may have milestones and deliverables all clustered toward the end of a very long project when it's too late to pivot toward a more successful outcome.

Anticipating Obstacles

Identifying obstacles is one of the primary purposes of a scrum daily standup. For workers in the middle of a sprint, obstacles interrupt the flow of heads-down work. By calling out blocker issues problems before they become interruptions, a manager may have the opportunity to intervene.

For example, if a user interface developer's next story involves substituting a designer's new icon family, and the designer hasn't supplied the icons, it's a blocker. The developer cannot complete the story without the icons. A manager or scrum master uses the forewarning to remind the designer that the team needs the icons, tout de suite.

If a consultant relies on employees for information and collaboration, it's important that these employees are available. Sometimes, either insufficient communication or unexpected higher priorities prevent employees from having the time to give a consultant. If these issues surface before they become obstacles, the sponsor can work with the consultant to rearrange the schedule or change the expectations.

Best Practices for Sponsoring a Successful Consulting Engagement

Following the practices in this checklist isn't a guarantee of success. However, *not following* these practices almost guarantees failure. These items are primarily the sponsor's responsibility.

Table 7.2 Best practices for sponsoring a consulting engagement

Practice	Explanation
Agree upon a detailed SOW	SOWs should identify the detailed specifics of work to be performed, well-placed milestones, well-defined deliverables, and a believable timeline. The company must pay close attention to the SOW and work with the consultant to ensure that it's mutually acceptable.
Support the consultant	A consultant may need to speak to or collaborate with busy employees. It's the sponsor's job to coordinate calendars to ensure employee availability issues don't scuttle the consultant's timeline and deliverables.

(Continues)

(*Continued*)

Practice	Explanation
Regularly provide feedback	Consulting engagements require active management to ensure the milestones are met and deliverables are useful. Although every consulting engagement requires significant managerial attention, the reward is the successful conclusion of the work.
Step in and change course when necessary	Regular milestones with managerial reviews or short SOWs enable the sponsor to alter the direction of the work, if necessary. Business needs may change during a consulting engagement or the consultant's discovery may suggest a pivot. An Agile approach of short iterations with deliverables helps protect the project's overall success even if it runs off course for a short period, needs to change course, or needs to address newly discovered issues.

Key Takeaways

1. Agile doesn't solve problems, so beware of conflating its powers. Before Agile practices can become useful, it's necessary to identify and address obstacles to success.

2. One of the most common business problems is *plateauing*—when a company stalls in a growth phase, it is often because it relies on business practices that no longer work.

3. Company growth provides opportunities to make radical changes in direction. Leaders must first consider improving their processes and practices and hire for skillsets missing on the current team.

4. A company's readiness for Agile requires frameworks for measurement of success and inter-team communications. A culture of learning and improvement is the key to Agile readiness.

5. Recognizing corporate dysfunction is easy, but an outsider may be the best solution.

6. Managerial squabbles, customer dissatisfaction and attrition, missed deadlines, and missed sales targets are clear indicators of problems requiring assistance from an outsider.

7. Consultants come in all shapes and sizes. Some consultants provide high-level advice, while others roll up their sleeves and work with teams to educate them and execute the work. Some do both. The nature of the company's problems dictates what to seek in a consultant.

8. Although the requirements for a consultant may differ by project, all consultants should possess experience, positivity, openness, and curiosity.

9. The person sponsoring the consultant must take a hands-on role to ensure the project's success. The managerial overhead required for any consulting project is an additional cost overlooked when computing the engagement costs.

10. To ensure the project's success and prevent misunderstandings, have a mutually agreed-upon detailed SOW, including milestones, deliverables, and dates.

CHAPTER 8

When Everything's in Place

What Works Best?

By now, the benefits of small-batch delivery should be clear. The muddiness of decomposing large problems into small, manageable pieces remains challenging. These tips and tricks are helpful in framing problems and tackling them head-on.

Small Multidisciplinary Teams

The concept of multidisciplinary teams sounds great on paper. Who doesn't love the idea of a cadre of experts banding together to solve gnarly problems? The reality of multidisciplinary teams may require some managerial attitude adjustment.

Authoritarian managers give orders and expect their minions to obey. In the mind of a dictatorial manager, everyone on their team must report directly to them for their *rule by fiat* to succeed. This way, the manager exerts full control over the project since each employee's livelihood depends on their performance. If this sounds retrograde and old-school, that's because it is.

One of the *Agile Manifesto* principles states, "Build projects around motivated individuals. Give them the environment and support they need and trust them to get the job done" (Beck et al. 2001).

The interpretation of this *Agile Manifesto* principle is that projects staffed with engaged people manage themselves. All a manager needs to do is provide the team with what they need to succeed and remove obstacles that stand in their way. While it's not precisely true that projects manage themselves, when the workers take responsibility for their deliverables, they also take on a large chunk of managerial responsibility.

Traditional managers occupy a special role in Agile projects. Managers are no longer directing the work or bossing people around. Instead, managers in Agile projects block and tackle, removing any threats to worker productivity. For example, if a Discovery team reaches an impasse where their lack of knowledge prevents them from fully understanding a customer's problem, a manager might find and hire an expert to work with the team.

Collaborative, Matrix Management

Matrix management is a business structure where employees have multiple bosses—one at the functional level and one or more at the project level. For example, an artist may answer to the head of Design at the *functional reporting* level. The artists on the Design team may share tips and tricks of the trade. The Design team manager is responsible for the members' performance reviews and other personnel issues. The artists on the Design team may also be farmed out to projects led by other managers. For example, the artist also may report to the head of Engineering on a multidisciplinary discovery project.

Answering to one boss is difficult enough. The prospect of simultaneously reporting to two or more bosses seems like too much bossing. The saving grace of this structure for Agile projects is the lightness of the Agile project bossing. There's little risk of an Agile project manager giving conflicting directions to a worker because the directions come from within the self-managing team.

A matrixed business structure demands collaboration at the managerial level. One of the greatest challenges of matrix management, regardless of the project's agility, is accurately gauging time requirements for each participant. Employees expected to contribute to multiple projects while participating in their functional group may feel tugged like rag dolls. It's almost always better for an employee to devote full attention to one project at a time. Companies that utilize matrix management often appoint an overseer, a Program Management Officer, to keep track of the interrelationships between projects and people.

Exploratory Mindset

To understand the exploratory mindset, it's easiest to start with the anti-exploratory mindset. Humans tend to mold facts to fit their under-standing. In the courts where justice is supposed to be blind, attorneys frequently *lead the witness*, putting words into witnesses' mouths. For example, a lawyer might ask a witness, "You didn't see the stop sign, did you?" instead of asking, "Did you see the stop sign?"

Although those in technical careers may consider themselves more honorable than lawyers, hubris is a human trait endemic to all profes-sions. Know-it-alls are so certain they already understand customers' problems, they'll toss out facts they learn that violate their understand-ing, considering them anomalies. For example, a Discovery team deter-mining how to make an intersection safer may be so intent on lowering the speed limit that they either ignore or disregard driver reports stating they entered the intersection with their view blocked by a large hedge on the street corner.

Exploratory teams must let the facts they learn drive their understand-ing. Furthermore, exploratory teams must question customers without leading them. This means that even if the team enters an engagement with preconceived notions, they must possess the intellectual honesty to toss these notions aside when the facts contradict them.

Appreciation of Waterfall

This book espouses the joys of Agile and the evils of Waterfall, so this isn't a last-chapter recantation. It's not a dream—Waterfall remains a failed methodology for most business endeavors.

Working in small Agile chunks to make targeted deliveries sometimes blinds project members to the big picture. Although it's anti-Agile to get too wrapped up in the big picture and get sucked into a large-scale design process, developing a conceptual picture of the whole is a nod to Waterfall.

Exploratory teams bridge the dichotomous Waterfall and Agile philos-ophies. An exploratory team has the time and mission to give projects a big think. Although exploratory teams should never fall into the Waterfall upfront design trap, they should gain a holistic enough understanding to make educated system-level recommendations. The members of exploratory teams aren't doing Waterfall, but they're not quite doing Agile either. This middle ground between the two methodologies offers a nod to Waterfall, but no more.

Applying Agile Across the Board

Agile methodologies are geared toward engineering projects. Using an Agile methodology in a non-engineering project requires some creativity and may necessitate taking some license with the rules.

The Agile *philosophy* expressed in the *Agile Manifesto* is perfectly well-suited to virtually any endeavor in a company. One of the *Agile Manifesto* principles, "Deliver working software frequently, from a couple of weeks to a couple of months, with a preference to the shorter timescale," is particularly applicable (Beck et al. 2001).

How Time-Boxing Benefits Everyone

The Agile principle of supplying small pieces of working software implies that deliverables are governed by time. When the time meter ends, the team delivers whatever it has completed.

Another approach is to regulate deliverables by functionality instead of time. The work cycle doesn't end with functionality-based deliverables until the team completes the agreed-upon features.

Ideally, a team fits all the required features into a reasonable and predictable timeframe. Realistically, if a Product Manager demands a deliverable on a specific date, she must negotiate with Engineering and choose which features can comfortably be finished by this date. If the Product Manager demands a feature-complete deliverable, she'll likely not have control of the delivery date.

Time-boxing, the governance of work by time constraints, is the preferred approach for Agile. In the best case, delivering working software is difficult. In the worst case, delivering working software is excruciating. The Agile way is to decompose large software projects into small pieces accomplishable in fixed timeframes.

The Agile concept of chipping away at a significant problem is so sensible, it's hard to imagine any business deliverable that wouldn't benefit from this approach. Granted, it's difficult to decompose every business problem into nice, neat two-week packages. Furthermore, even if a team is clever enough to break a big problem into small pieces, finding an equivalent of working software that encompasses the work of non-software-delivering teams is another challenge.

Not Everything Fits Into Short Iterations—A Sales Use Case

Sales doesn't lend itself to Agile processes like time-boxing in short iterations and delivering working results. The sales cycle may take years when the company's product is complex, cloud-based enterprise software. Although cultivating a sales prospect is a long-term affair, even a sales organization may benefit from Agile.

A sales pipeline review perfectly fits an Agile approach. Anyone involved in sales has experienced hot prospects cooling off and cold prospects heating up. Sometimes the leaderboard of potential sales is like a race with horses coming up from the back. Sales must be nimble enough to change course as prospects ebb and flow. Doggedly sticking to a plan that's no longer relevant is waterfall-ish. Pivoting when sales conditions change is agile.

A sales forecast is the most consequential document a company produces. Typically, the head of Sales collaborates with the Chief Financial Officer (CFO), CEO, and other executives in the last quarter of the fiscal year to create a forecast for the next year. A company relies on the sales forecast for most of its financial decisions, including:

1. **Hiring plan**—A sales forecast comes with caveats. For example, Sales will achieve X in revenue if the company rolls out product Y in Q2. A hiring plan specifies the roles that must be filled to deliver product Y in Q2.

2. **Bonus plan**—Most companies with bonus plans designate part of the payout to personal performance and part of the payout to company performance. Employees who underperform and receive nothing for their personal performance bonus may still receive a payout if the company meets or exceeds its sales goal.

3. **Capital and operational expenditures**—Anticipated revenue determines how much the company will spend on laptops, facilities, hosting, and other costly items.

Companies use a sales forecast to guide growth, acceleration, and
spending. The impact of a sales forecast is immense. Yet, a sales forecast
is, at best, an educated guess.

Sales may use its pipeline to guess at the likely deals that will close
each quarter. Each deal in the pipeline has a revenue target, a target close
date, and a probability of successfully closing. CFOs are skilled at taking
these numbers and producing a revenue target that's neither too aggressive nor too conservative. Sometimes, a nearly sure-thing deal falls apart
and a long-shot deal miraculously closes. If the sales pipeline is large
enough, the CFO's probabilistic model may remain mostly correct even
with the inevitable good and bad surprises.

Since a company bases growth, acceleration, and spending on the sales
forecast, under-forecasting sales is nearly as damaging as over-forecasting
sales. If sales exceed the forecast, the company may not accelerate quickly
enough. If sales are significantly less than the forecast, the company may
spend too much and be unable to meet its payroll.

Producing a sales forecast feels closer to Waterfall than Agile. A team
assiduously works to generate the forecast and hands it off to the rest of
the company as the basis for growth and spending plans. Yet, there's little
point in forecasting an entire year's sales when accurately predicting sales
for the next three months is a crapshoot.

Here's an example of a more Agile approach to forecasting and
planning:

1. Sales and the CFO generate a sales forecast for the next quarter.
   Since the forecast covers a smaller and more immediate timeframe,
   the level of effort to create the report isn't nearly as great as producing
   a forecast for the year.
2. The other company executives review the plans and determine
   a quarterly budget for hiring, raises, capital expenditures, and
   operational expenditures.

3. The CEO restructures the bonus plan to have four smaller payouts instead of one large payout at the end of the fiscal year. Focusing on a narrower timespan than a year solves the problem of bonus incentives established at the beginning of the year becoming obsolete as business needs change.

4. Sales and the CFO regularly review the sales forecast, making changes to reflect reality. Budgetary items are adjusted to match the changes in the forecast.

5. Over the course of a year, a company inevitably faces unexpected business challenges and opportunities. The constant forecast and budget review cycle enables a company to pivot to address these challenges and opportunities. For example, a large sales prospect will likely sign a deal if the company integrates with a scheduling service. Although the scheduling service integration isn't on the product roadmap, Product Management believes this integration will drive sales to other prospective customers. Therefore, the CEO may choose to forgo some profit in a quarter and instead hire an additional engineer for the integration work.

Managing an Agile Company

Agile teams are self-managing. So, there's no need for managers, right? Wrong.

Managers in Agile companies are still important. Regardless of agility, employees always require mentorship, support, and an ear for their concerns and issues. From a workday perspective, however, the role of an Agile manager differs from the norm in non-Agile companies.

Self-managing team members determine how they will work to meet customer expectations and deadlines. The team determines the methodology that best suits its needs, how its estimates work, and how work assignments are distributed.

The intense focus of Agile teams provides enormous benefits as well as some pitfalls. Intensely focusing on a goal necessitates ignoring everything else. Although a team may work in isolation to complete its work, customer delivery requires coordination between multiple teams.

Managers are important in ensuring that multiple Engineering teams are in sync, that Marketing and Sales are aware of Engineering and Product Management deliverables, and that Customer Support is informed about product changes.

Although a manager must ensure the company's various parts work collaboratively, this is not management's foremost responsibility. The key responsibility of management is to determine and communicate the teams' priorities. A secondary, but equally important, managerial role is to monitor progress against objectives and to act when objectives are in jeopardy.

Agile Management

This book focuses on applying Agile principles from software development to a company's non-engineering disciplines. Since management's role in an Agile company is less about bossing employees and more about clearing the way for self-managing teams to flourish, it seems logical that management adopt Agile practices.

Not so fast. It's a stretch to take the *Agile Manifesto* philosophy and twist it to apply to managerial duties. Instead, management may adopt a more focused and nimble approach to monitoring and directing that's more akin to lowercase agility. *Reminder:* Uppercase Agile refers to the practices of the *Agile Manifesto* and lowercase agile refers to sprightliness.

In her 2021 book, *Radical Focus*, Christina Wodtke gives a suggestion for more nimble management. She espouses that each manager prepares a four-quadrant, one-page document for weekly alignment meetings (Wodtke 2021, 54).

The quadrants contain the following information:

Quadrant 1—This Week's Priorities

- Label each item P1 for top priority or P2 for secondary priority.
- Exclude items that are neither top nor second priority.
- This quadrant holds the few things prioritized for this week.

Quadrant 2—Objectives and KRs

- List the key objectives. It's okay if there's just one objective. In fact, having one objective identified as the most important item is preferable to identifying a bunch of objectives as all top priority (P1).
- List up to three KRs per objective.
- Place a confidence number next to each KR (on a scale of 1 to 10). A 5/10 indicates 50 percent confidence.
- Don't waste time discussing high-confidence KRs.
- If the confidence level of a KR decreases from the previous week, it should be a topic of conversation.

Quadrant 3—Next Four Weeks

- Identify essential items that will be important in the near-ish term.
- These items may fall outside a team's objectives but require attention, nonetheless.
- The purpose of this quadrant is for alignment between teams. If there's a big product release next month, it's time for Marketing, Sales, Product, Engineering, and Customer Success to sync up.

Quadrant 4—Health Metrics

- Pick a few things you want to heed as you seek to hit your objectives. These are the things you can't afford to mess up. Items like these are appropriate for this quadrant: technical debt acquisition or paydown, key customer relationships, morale, and burnout.
- These items represent key performance indicators for the business.
- Provide general metrics that might or might not tie into the OKRs.

Rethinking Management Meetings

Managers bemoan the time spent in meetings but are often the instigators of meeting-itis. Occasionally, however, participants leave meetings feeling the time was well-spent. In successful meetings, the participants meet their objectives in the least amount of time. Effective meetings must have agendas that lay out the goals and a facilitator to move things along. Enlightened companies encourage employees to decline meetings in which they will have no meaningful impact on the agenda.

One of the trickiest types of meetings is when management convenes to update each other. These alignment meetings tend to go awry because one manager's updates are seldom useful to the other managers. These meetings waste highly paid employees' time.

The presence of C-suite executives in management meetings further degrades these meetings because managers often use their time to tout accomplishments instead of raising red flags. Highlighting successes is easy to communicate in an e-mail or Slack message because it requires no discussion. The true value of a management meeting derives from honest discussion of difficult topics like unhappy customers, jeopardized goals, and employee attrition. A management meeting becomes engaging and effective if the team puts politics aside and collaborates to solve problems.

If each manager comes to a management meeting with a four-quadrant document, they're already off to a great start. The short time required to prepare the four quadrants forces a manager to think about the immediate, the longer term, and the obstacles they may face along the way.

By focusing on controversial topics like objectives in jeopardy or organizational health problems, managers will naturally collaborate to ameliorate the problems. Even though a naïve CEO may sleep soundly after *happy path* meetings, realistic CEOs will appreciate it when managers raise problems and find solutions.

Participants will be thankful they prepared in advance and used the time to discuss only substantive issues when the meetings are efficient and agenda-driven.

Identifying Conflicting Objectives

In the best of companies, objectives are transparent, so each department knows the other departments' primary goals. Even if objectives are transparent, other groups often don't absorb them.

For example, a Sales team goal might be to make deep inroads into Samsung's customer base. This goal may have a KR that specifies bolstering the feature set of the Android mobile app. If Engineering aims to deliver an iOS (Apple) mobile app without attention to the Android side, it's a case of conflicting objectives. Moreover, this type of disconnect between teams causes bad blood because neither side feels supported by their counterparts.

Left unchecked, suppose Sales makes good on its objective and sells deep into Samsung's customer base. The next step is an urgent request from Sales for Engineering to beef up its Android support. Unless Engineering drops its iOS work and capitulates to the demands of Sales, the company risks taking on new, disgruntled customers.

Although this disconnect between Sales and Engineering may sound fictitious, it's all too common when a company doesn't continually revisit objectives. Conflicting objectives cause Engineering to accuse Sales of peddling vaporware and causes Sales to accuse Engineering of sandbagging.

Introducing four-quadrant management documents in alignment meetings exposes conflicting objectives so they can be nipped in the bud before interdepartmental warfare ensues.

Developing an Agile Managerial Mindset

Regardless of one's feelings about fast food and McDonald's, the Golden Arches provides a helpful management example. McDonald's management training requires intimate knowledge of a store's workstations. In a pinch, McDonald's managers are so well-trained, they can make milkshakes, flip burgers, prepare fries, or operate the cash register. An informed suggestion is likely forthcoming when an employee brings a problem to a McDonald's manager.

Ideally, company managers possess more than a passing understanding of their employee's jobs. Company managers should follow the

McDonald's model where Engineering managers are former engineers, and Sales leaders are former salespeople.

Do self-managing Agile teams obviate the need for well-informed, McDonald's-style managers? Nope, deeply knowledgeable managers are still invaluable, but their contributions are somewhat different in Agile companies.

Sometimes managers who know everything about their employees' jobs *micromanage*, becoming too involved in the work's minutiae in an unhelpful manner. For example, instead of answering a question about milkshake composition, a McDonald's manager might go make the shakes herself. Although the manager may have solved the immediate problem, they neglected to teach the employee. Consequently, the same problem will likely recur. Similarly, a VP of Engineering ideally knows enough to understand the team's code but allows the team leaders to run the code reviews. A micromanaging manager risks losing sight of the big picture because of low-level distractions.

Managers in self-managing Agile companies are less prone to micromanage. However, when a team hits roadblocks that jeopardize achieving its objectives, a knowledgeable manager asks the right questions and provides valuable advice.

Bringing It All Together … and Two Confessions

For those who read this book seeking ways to deliver work products faster, here's my first confession: Agile does not accelerate work schedules nor facilitates speedier output. The good news is that teams produce better results in the same amount of time.

Even if Agile doesn't produce faster delivery, breaking large problems into smaller more understandable pieces results in more accurate estimates. Furthermore, the results of the circular process of planning, developing, seeking feedback, and fine-tuning are work products that address immediate customer problems better than non-Agile approaches. Still, customers will always bemoan the time it takes to receive their solutions. Hopefully, their satisfaction with Agile-fueled results allays their annoyance at the wait.

Agile replaces the Waterfall process. Waterfall is especially ill-suited to work that's inexpensive to tweak when things go awry. Besides those in building construction, few work mistakes are prohibitively expensive to fix.

Even mission-critical applications like rocket launches, which may result in loss of life, employ Agile approaches, albeit accompanied by sophisticated and thorough automated testing processes.

Agile is now over 20—young for a person, but long in the tooth for a business philosophy. Humans are wired to seek a better mousetrap. Dissatisfaction with Agile is causing some to consider post-Agile philosophies. In many cases, however, the argument is not with the eminently sensible *Agile Manifesto*, but with the Agile methodologies, which were invented to help teams apply the Agile philosophy.

Many teams cloak themselves in the terminology of Scrum—sprints, standups, backlogs, retrospectives—while working in a Waterfall mode. Unfortunately, adopting the trappings of Agile methodologies without understanding the Agile philosophy is talking the talk without walking the walk. No wonder Agile gets a bad rap!

My second confession: The world would be better if Agile methodologies were never invented. Teams are better served by going to the original text of the *Agile Manifesto* than embracing the abstractions offered by Agile methodologies. Granted, figuring out how to apply the Agile philosophy to the daily work of a company is a heavy lift. But the prospect of replacing mediocre with stellar work products makes the Agile struggle worthwhile.

Every successful company with a great business model faces the same problem: Customers become so invested in their products that they demand more than the company can easily deliver. Demanding customers is the best problem any company can have. These insistent customers also understand that exquisite solutions aren't easy, quick, or cheap. By developing Agile processes across the enterprise, companies can respond to demand with realistic plans and schedules while including customers in the decision-making and evaluation.

Corporate Agility: A Smooth Ride Forevermore or a Constant Struggle?

The journey to spread the *Agile Manifesto* philosophy across the organization is far from linear. Although a *journey* is defined as the act of going from one place to another, the word implies that important things happen during the trip.

Conceptually, the journey begins in Waterfall-land and ends in Agile-land. Realistically, most companies don't begin with strict Waterfall and don't end with strict Agile. Consequently, most companies travel a circuitous route with plenty of twists and turns.

The *Agile Manifesto* was penned by software luminaries seeking a better way to work. The Agile methodologies that followed are mostly intended for Engineering teams. Interestingly, Engineering teams struggle with adopting the elements of Agile, even though the philosophy and methodologies were purpose-built for them.

Understanding Agile principles well enough to apply them to non-engineering corporate projects requires both creativity and a clear understanding of the *Agile Manifesto* philosophy. Individuals and teams develop Agile muscles by absorbing the philosophy and making forays into small-batch deliverables in time-boxed iterations.

Despite the best efforts of the purveyors of Agile methodologies to prescribe behavior, Agile is a constant challenge. By keeping at it through repetition and commitment, Agile muscles will transform into an Agile habit. Teammates demonstrate their Agile habit when they naturally look for ways to apply the *Agile Manifesto* philosophy. Team members learn from the twists of their Agile journey and apply their newfound knowledge at every turn.

Key Takeaways

1. Traditional managerial roles change with self-managing Agile teams. Managers become facilitators, obstacle-removers, and less bossy.
2. Small, multidisciplinary discovery teams imply a matrix-managed business structure.
3. Matrix management has its challenges when employees answer to multiple managers. Ideally, employees focus on a single project at a time.
4. The exploratory mindset requires team members to leave their preconceptions at the door and listen closely to customers without asking leading questions.

5. Time-boxing is a key Agile practice that benefits just about any project.

6. Although not everything fits neatly into a short work-cycle, the results are often better when large projects are decomposed into small pieces.

7. Management is generally not an Agile endeavor, but managers can certainly act with agility.

8. Managers become agile by running efficient meetings and eliminating unnecessary meetings.

9. A four-quadrant document allows managers to identify and discuss short- and longer-term problem areas in alignment meetings.

10. Agile isn't easy, but developing the proper musculature leads to an Agile habit.

Glossary

Agile Manifesto: A seminal software development philosophy penned in 2001 by a group of legendary software developers at a Wasatch Mountain, Utah ski resort. The Agile Manifesto refutes an earlier approach to software called *Waterfall*, in which work is performed in discrete stages and handed off to the next team upon completion. Instead, the Agile Manifesto prescribes a more collaborative work style with fewer handoffs.

Agile programming: Although Agile isn't a programming style, the Agile approach to software development implies decomposing large problems into smaller ones, working on them in short iterations, and soliciting user feedback after each iteration.

Average pages per visit: A measure of the pages visited by individual website visitors averaged over the total number of visitors to the website. The number of pages website visitors click on is an excellent measure of the site's engagement. When the pages per visit increase, it reflects more interesting and engaging content.

Backlog: A Scrum term referring to the set of user stories not scheduled in a sprint.

Bounce rate: The bounce rate measures the percentage of people who land on a website, don't interact, and leave. Website designers work to reduce bounce rates.

Code commit: When a programmer submits software to a version control system, the act of committing the code often precipitates a series of prescribed behaviors, including code review, the automated building of the software, and the automated execution of tests.

Continuous delivery: An automated process that enables teams to deploy software to targeted environments after a code commit.

Continuous integration: An automated process that builds software and runs tests, typically in a test environment, whenever code is committed to a source code repository.

Extreme Programming: A technically focused Agile methodology that includes pair programming, test-driven development, continuous integration, and continuous delivery. Extreme Programming is difficult to adapt to non-engineering projects.

Failing fast: Quickly recognizing when an idea or an approach isn't succeeding before too much time, effort, and money is wasted.

Fire: A customer emergency requiring company employees to drop everything they're doing to focus on extinguishing the blaze. Too much firefighting derails planned deliverable dates.

Functional reporting: A traditional reporting structure where an employee reports to a manager based on role. For example, a team of quality engineers reports functionally to the head of Quality, but each may be farmed out to project teams managed by someone else. Typically, one's functional manager handles personnel issues like performance reviews. In a matrix-managed structure, an employee has a single functional manager and one or more project managers.

Git: A distributed version control system that tracks file changes and supports teams of programmers.

GitHub: Cloud-based hosting service for software development and version control using the Git version control system.

Kanban: An Agile methodology based on a Japanese manufacturing system in which the capacity of workers on the assembly line regulates the supply of components.

Lean development: An Agile methodology incorporating lean manufacturing principles of minimizing waste and maximizing value.

Management by objectives: A theory devised by Peter Drucker in 1954 promoting manager/employee goals that are reviewed annually.

Matrix management: A business structure where employees have multiple bosses—one at the functional level and one or more at the project level.

Methodology: The specification of transforming a philosophy like the *Agile Manifesto* into an actionable set of behaviors.

Micromanagement: Becoming too involved in the minutiae of the work in a manner that's unhelpful to the employee.

Objectives and key results (OKRs): A management methodology that helps ensure everyone in a company is focusing their efforts on the same important issues. Devised by Intel President and CEO, Andy Grove, and popularized by John Doerr, Venture Capitalist at Kleiner Perkins, OKRs are implemented at Google, Facebook, and other leading software companies.

Pair programming: An Extreme Programming practice where two programmers work together to write or modify a piece of code.

Postmortem: Borrowed from forensics, a software postmortem is a report issued after a fire that explains the root causes and intended actions to prevent a recurrence.

Process heaviness: When complicated tools or excessive bureaucracy get in the way of achieving goals. The selection of appropriate tools and processes may help facilitate progress. It's a sign of process heaviness when a team must change how it performs its work to satisfy the requirements of the tool.

Research spike: An Agile methodology salve that blocks time for learning and doesn't result in a customer-deliverable product.

Retrospective: A Scrum practice where a team reflects on the positives and negatives of a completed sprint.

Scope creep: A common practice where additional work is added after stakeholders have agreed on the parameters of a work iteration.

Scrum: The most widely practiced Agile methodology. Scrum utilizes user stories, story points, sprints, retrospectives, and backlog. Scrum is so ubiquitous as an Agile methodology that *Scrum* and *Agile* are frequently used interchangeably; this is incorrect. Scrum includes a set of practices that help teams follow an Agile philosophy.

Scrumban: A blending of Agile methodologies that use elements of Scrum and Kanban.

SEO: Search engine optimization is the process used to optimize a website's technical configuration. SEO enables a website's pages to become easily findable and higher ranked by search engines.

Sponsor: A company employee who manages a consulting engagement. Typically, a sponsor acts as a sounding board for ideas, an offensive lineman to clear the way for the consultant to learn, and someone to hold them to task.

Sprint: The active phase of a Scrum cycle where the team works headsdown for a short duration, typically a couple of weeks. The goal of a sprint is to produce working software at the end.

Story points: A measure of the complexity of a story. Story points may use whatever measurement scale the team decides but points must be assigned consistently across sprints.

Technical debt: The accrual of shortcuts and workarounds to meet deadlines. Technical debt may cause future problems if substandard work is never corrected and keeps piling up.

Test-driven development (TDD): An Extreme Programming practice where tests are written before code is written. TDD implies that the programmer has a complete enough understanding of the problem to know how the code should behave.

Time-boxing: Limiting work to a specified period. Sprints are typically time-boxed to a couple of weeks, and the delivered functionality reflects whatever can fit into the box. The alternative to time-boxing is for teams to work until a feature set is completed, regardless of time.

User stories: The basic unit of work of a Scrum sprint. Stories express the *who*, *what*, and *why* but don't provide excessive detail. Stories spark discussion to ensure all parties understand and agree on the details.

Velocity: The sum of the completed story points in a sprint. The averaging of completed story points over many sprints provides an average team velocity. Note that any changes to the team like additions, subtractions, or swaps of people results in velocity changes.

Waterfall: A development approach with lengthy periods of design, documentation, development, and testing. When one group finishes, the work is handed off for the next group to begin. Waterfall and Agile are diametrically opposed processes.

Work in progress (WIP): A Kanban concept governing work so that individuals must complete existing work before undertaking new work.

References

Beck, K., B. Mike, A. van Bennekum, A. Cockburn, W. Cunningham, M. Fowler, J. Grenning, et al. 2001. "Manifesto for Agile Software Development." https://agilemanifesto.org/ (accessed April 2022).

Beck, K., B. Mike, A. van Bennekum, A. Cockburn, W. Cunningham, M. Fowler, J. Grenning, et al. 2001. "Principles Behind the Agile Manifesto." https://agilemanifesto.org/principles.html (accessed April 2022).

Brand Minds. 2018. "Why Did Kodak Fail and What Can You Learn From Its Demise." https://brand-minds.medium.com/why-did-kodak-fail-and-what-can-you-learn-from-its-failure-70b92793493c (accessed May 2022).

DesiLu Productions. 1956. "Lucy and the Chocolate Factory." www.youtube.com/watch?v=NkQ58I53mjk (accessed May 2022).

Doerr, J. 2018. *Measure What Matters: How Google, Bono, and the Gates Foundation Rock the World With OKRs.* New York, NY: Portfolio/Penguin.

Drucker, P. 1954. *The Practice of Management.* New York, NY: Harper Collins Publishers, Inc.

Fahy, R., B. Evarts, and G.P. Stein. 2022. "National Fire Protection Association's US Fire Department Profile." www.nfpa.org/News-and-Research/Data-research-and-tools/Emergency-Responders/US-fire-department-profile#:~:text=Key%20findings,firefighters%20were%20female%20(9%25) (accessed June 2022).

Google. 2020. "Google's OKR Playbook." www.whatmatters.com/resources/google-okr-playbook (accessed July 2022).

Hern, A. 2018. "The Two-Pizza Rule and the Secret of Amazon's Success." www.theguardian.com/technology/2018/apr/24/the-two-pizza-rule-and-the-secret-of-amazons-success (accessed August 2022).

Highsmith, J. 2001. "History: The Agile Manifesto." https://agilemanifesto.org/history (accessed September 2022).

Isaacson, W. 2017. *Leonardo Da Vinci.* New York, NY: Simon & Schuster.

Lavallee, G. 2022. "You Can't Code Your Way Out of the Culture Problem." https://slate.com/technology/2022/11/elon-musk-twitter-code-fixation.html (accessed September 2022).

Marxist Internet Archive. n.d. "Chapter IV. Position of the Communists in Relation to the Various Existing Opposition Parties." www.marxists.org/archive/marx/works/1848/communist-manifesto/ch04.htm (accessed September 12, 2022).

ProductPlan.com. 2022. "Lean Software Development." www.productplan.com/glossary/lean-software-development/ (accessed July 2022).

Schwartz, A. and A. Hurst. 2022. "Is Texting and Driving Illegal?" www
.policygenius.com/auto-insurance/texting-and-driving-laws-in-all-50-states/
(accessed October 2022).

Scrum.org. 2022. "The Scrum Framework." www.scrum.org/resources/what-is-
scrum (accessed August 2022).

Wodtke, C. 2021. *Radical Focus: Achieving Your Most Important Goals With
Objectives and Key Results*. Cucina Media LLC.

About the Author

David Asch has a 36-year career in startup and mid-stage commercial software companies. David began as a Software Developer for the first part of his career and subsequently moved into management, leading technical teams for over 20 years. He's worked in various industries, including transportation, supply chain, retail analytics, scientific marketing, blockchain, and secure communications.

In virtually all his managerial positions, David produced robust, enterprise software-as-a-service products in cloud-based environments. He introduced Agile philosophy and methodologies to each of his companies, enabling his teams to meet their goals.

David founded 10xPrinciples, a management/organizational consulting company, to help technology companies navigate the transition from startup to mid-stage. During this time of rapid growth and change, teams typically find that the *wearing many hats* culture from their startup days is no longer the best approach to honoring commitments. David helps these companies weave Agile practices into the fabric of their cultures.

Before 10xPrinciples, David was Vice President of Product Development at Decisiv. He managed a large, distributed organization with employees scattered throughout the United States and near-shore consultants in Argentina and Costa Rica. Instead of separating teams by geography, David blended the teams using digital communication and collaboration tools. By introducing Extreme Programming methodologies, including test automation, automatic deployment, and pair programming, David reduced the release cycle from six weeks to weekly deployments.

In a prior position as Director of Engineering at Sentrana, David faced an entirely different problem. In addition to managing a U.S. team, David was responsible for two large engineering teams in Bangladesh. David introduced the Bangladesh teams to the Scrum methodology and taught the teams about stories, sprints, velocity, and retrospectives. The introduction of Scrum also changed how the U.S. team communicated with the Bangladesh team; since the teams were so far apart geographically and culturally, the U.S. team learned to clearly communicate their ideas graphically, using prototyping to ensure both sides were aligned.

David's recognized expertise in companywide Agile-driven management makes him invaluable to clients who need to implement Agile principles and methodologies into their unique business environments.

Index

Printed in the USA
CPSIA information can be obtained
at www.ICGtesting.com
CBHW072042251124
17873CB00008B/291